Wrestle Like A Girl

WRESTLE LIKE A GIRL

Copyright © 2016 By Craig Sesker and Jamie Moffatt

All rights reserved. This book, or parts thereof, may not be reproduced in any form without permission from the publisher.

Published by Exit Zero Publishing
www.exitzero.us

Book design by Jack Wright
Cover design by Jackie Valori

Cover photo credits: Tony Rotundo, John Sachs and Larry Slater

Back cover photo by Larry Slater

First edition: October, 2016
Second printing: December, 2023

ISBN 978-0-9972662-0-7

Thank you to the sponsors of this book
Andy Barth / Jamie Moffatt / Wrestle Like A Girl, Inc.

Contents

FOREWORD	**Sally Roberts, WLAG**	8
CHAPTER 1	**Jackpot in Vegas: The 2015 Worlds**	12
CHAPTER 2	**Afsoon Roshanzamir & Marie Ziegler**	16
CHAPTER 3	**Tricia Saunders**	32
CHAPTER 4	**Iris Smith**	42
CHAPTER 5	**Kristie Marano**	50
CHAPTER 6	**Athens: The 2004 Olympics**	62
CHAPTER 7	**Coach Terry Steiner**	78
CHAPTER 8	**Beijing: The 2008 Olympics**	92
CHAPTER 9	**Elena Pirozhkova**	100
CHAPTER 10	**London: The 2012 Olympics**	110
CHAPTER 11	**The Fight to Stay in the Games**	122
CHAPTER 12	**Leigh Jaynes**	128
CHAPTER 13	**Adeline Gray**	136
CHAPTER 14	**Helen Maroulis**	148
CHAPTER 15	**Rio de Janeiro: The 2016 Olympics**	158

Dedicated to Dr. Kirsten Ashley Moffatt, Ph.D
(1969-2016)
You made us so proud all of your life.

In the fall of 1985, Kirsten Moffatt was a junior at Chatfield High School in Littleton, Colorado. She went to the varsity wrestling coach before the first day of practice and asked if she could join the team. "Sorry, only boys are permitted on the wrestling team," she was abruptly told.

Twenty years later, Adeline Gray, a Junior at Chatfield, captained the school's wrestling team. She went on to become a multiple-time World champion wrestler.

Wrestle Like A Girl

foreword
By SALLY ROBERTS / WRESTLE LIKE A GIRL

Wrestle Like A Girl (WLAG) was founded by Sally Roberts, a two-time World bronze medalist and three-time National champion, to help empower and educate girls and women across the United States through the sport of wrestling. The non-profit 501(c)3 organization is headquartered in Colorado Springs, Colorado and is a sponsor and the distribution center for this book. Further information on WLAG can be found at wrestlelikeagirl.org.

Women's wrestling has come a long way since its inception at the first World Championships in 1987 in Lorenskog, Norway. As of 2023, female wrestlers in high school now number nearly 55,000 across America; over 44 states recognize girls' high school wrestling as an official sport; and 165 colleges and universities offer varsity wrestling programs for women. As the women's wrestling landscape expands, safe spaces for female wrestlers are expanding, as evidenced by Delaware State University's collaboration with the HBCU Wrestling Initiative and Wrestle Like a Girl. This initiative provides educational opportunities for girls and women of color, and signifies a crucial step toward recognizing girls' high school wrestling as an official sport in Delaware.

The American collegiate wrestling system is growing, creating opportunities for girls and women to access financial, social and educational mobility. Stakeholders, such as USA Wrestling, NCAA and NAIA, have expanded opportunities for women in collegiate wrestling. Title IX promises equal opportunities in education and sports, and has empowered women in the United States while influencing global conversations about women's sports. Without the support of policies and stakeholders, it is possible my voice would not be amplifying the plight of our girls and women, both in sport and beyond, who are often overlooked, invisible, and without voice or representation.

With women's wrestling being an Olympic freestyle sport, we're enabling girls worldwide to come to the U.S., wrestle and return home educated and empowered. However, continued Title IX enforcement is crucial, as many institutions still neglect women's sports.

As USA Wrestling's National Team coach Terry Steiner said in his call to action, "You ask the question — why women's wrestling? I ask you the question — why NOT women's wrestling? We can all agree on one thing: Wrestling is a great sport! And it is an even better teacher of life skills." Women's wrestling embodies the democratic spirit of fairness, opportunity and work ethic. It nurtures confidence and character, fostering innovation and entrepreneurship. Women's participation and partnership are vital in peacekeeping, diplomacy and national security. Empowering women is essential for societal success and is the 21st century's foremost task.

The tides are turning in favor of women's wrestling. Heroines like Helen Maroulis and Tamyra Mensah-Stock have made history, displaying courage, persistence and resilience. They are role models for girls from all walks of life, from refugees to those from broken homes. My singular focus in life are these girls and this sport. I know what it's like to fight, and I know what it's like to fight for what you love.

Throughout this book, you will find more than just stories of women dominating the mat. You will find more than lessons on winning matches. You will find the grit that makes women overcomers and forces to be reckoned with. These women are my sisters; I am honored to be included among them. They exemplify champions in life and in sport, inspiring us to flourish, trust ourselves — and become legends..

The only (so far...) U.S. women's wrestling team to win the World Championship

The U.S. 1999 women's World team: Rob Eiter (head coach), Tricia Saunders, Kristie Marano, Sandra Bacher, Lauren Lamb, Tina George, Stephanie Murata and Mike Duroe (USA Wrestling national coach).

CHAPTER 1
Jackpot in Vegas: The 2015 Worlds

The stage was set for a historic, landmark and festive night for women's freestyle wrestling. The 5,000-seat Orleans Arena was packed to capacity as American flags were passionately waved throughout the sparkling Las Vegas venue. The atmosphere was electric as fans gathered in anticipation for the medal round of the World Wrestling Championships on September 11, 2015.

Just over a quarter-century after American women took a chance on a brand new and completely unknown sport at the 1989 World Championships in a small Switzerland city, the sport of women's freestyle wrestling demonstrated just how far it had advanced and evolved.

The sport was being showcased in the entertainment capital of the world in Las Vegas, Nevada.

Shortly into the session, it was time for the gold-medal bout at 55 kilograms/121 pounds.

First out of the tunnel and onto the main arena floor was 2014 World silver medalist Irina Ologonova of Russia.

And then it was time for United World Wrestling public address announcer Jason Bryant to introduce Ologonova's opponent...

"And from the United States of America, Hel-ennn Ma-roooo-lis."

The roar was deafening as the patriotic crowd clapped and cheered in support of Helen Maroulis, who had previously placed second and third in the World.

The whistle blew to start the match and Maroulis was quickly in on the attack. The silky-smooth technique and cat-like quickness of Maroulis was immediately apparent.

She peppered her Russian oppo-

Helen Maroulis celebrates her first World championship title in 2015. Tony Rotundo

nent with an aggressive approach, scoring on an array of leg attacks en route to a dominating 11-0 technical fall win.

A beaming Maroulis ran around the mat holding an American flag above her head in celebration of her breakthrough victory.

She had captured her first World title.

"The crowd was incredible," Maroulis said after her victory. "I was excited before every match because I knew the crowd was going to be cheering. Every coach I've ever had since I was seven years old was in the stands. I was just so excited. I couldn't wait to walk out of the tunnel and get on the mat and just wrestle. It's just been great to have the World Championships here in Las Vegas."

An hour and a half later, the crowd was buzzing again in anticipation of another USA finalist. And another potential gold medal.

First out of the tunnel was 2014 World bronze medalist Qian Zhou of China.

And then came another thundering announcement from Bryant over the PA...

"And from the United States of America, Ade-line Grayyyyyy."

The crowd erupted again as flags waved while a loud, booming chant of "U-S-A, U-S-A" bounced off the arena walls.

Adeline Gray walked up the stairs and strode confidently onto the elevated platform. She clapped her hands as she prepared for her third World finals match in the past four years, but her first on American soil.

The unflappable Gray actually gave up the match's first takedown, but kept her composure. She eventually took control in the second period by turning Zhou and nearly pinning her before finishing off the win with a series of leg laces as the crowd stood and cheered.

She ran around the mat holding an American flag above her head in celebration of her triumph. She then waved to the crowd as a huge smile spread across her face. "I don't think there's a girl out there who can beat me," Gray said that night. "It's just about stepping on that mat and making sure I'm disciplined enough to get my job done that day. If I stay healthy, I think I can win."

It was Gray's third World title after she had earlier won championships in 2012 and 2014.

"I'm ready to win the Olympics," Gray said. "I can't wait to have that opportunity."

To round out the U.S. medal count, Leigh Jaynes earned a bronze at 60 kilograms/132 pounds by edging Irina Natreba on criteria, 4-4, to give the team three medals in total.

By crowning a pair of gold medalists at the 2015 World Championships, the U.S. sent a resounding message to the rest of the World. Team USA was serious about winning gold medals in women's wrestling at the 2016 Olympic Games in Rio de Janeiro, Brazil.

Women's freestyle had made its debut at the 2004 Olympics and the U.S. fell just short of a gold medal in Athens, Greece, with Sara McMann capturing a silver medal.

The Americans came up short of

Adeline Gray wins her third World championship title in 2015. Tony Rotundo

the finals in 2008 in Beijing, China and in 2012 in London, England. Randi Miller won a bronze medal in 2008 and Clarissa Chun earned a bronze medal in 2012.

The American women were determined and confident they would change their fortunes at the 2016 Olympics.

Female wrestlers had endured a long, tough and grueling road in pursuit of the ultimate achievement in their sport, an Olympic gold medal for the United States of America.

CHAPTER 2
Afsoon Roshanzamir & Marie Ziegler

The first time Marie Ziegler saw Afsoon Roshanzamir was in 1988 in Reno, Nevada. Ziegler was there watching her boyfriend compete in a high school wrestling tournament.

"I vividly recall there being a big crowd gathering around one of the mats because a girl was wrestling. It turned out the girl was Afsoon," Ziegler said. "I was intrigued, and kind of in awe. What stood out to me was that she was very good. She really knew how to wrestle."

A year later, Ziegler and Roshanzamir met each other for the first time.

Women's wrestling was going to be included at the 1989 World Championships, and the first U.S. World Team Training Camp was being held in Concord, California.

Just three people were there for the start of that first camp — Ziegler, Roshanzamir and Coach Rusty Davidson.

"We were thrown into this new situation that was different and unheard of," said Ziegler. "It was unchartered territory and we were both trying to figure it out. We were both trying to navigate this. We didn't know what we were doing — we just knew we were there to do *something*."

Lee Allen, a U.S. Olympian, had organized an international women's wrestling tournament in San Francisco in 1989.

The highest American finisher at that event would represent the U.S. at the 1989 World Championships.

By that time, Roshanzamir was a very accomplished wrestler and was the highest American finisher at 47 kilograms/103.5 pounds. Ziegler was a newcomer at 44 kilograms/97 pounds one win away from making history in Martigny, Switzerland

Roshanzamir had followed a long and often scary path to reach that point in her life. She was born on August 16, 1972, the only child of an Iranian champion wrestler, Manouchehr "Manu" Roshanzamir. Wrestling is the national sport in Iran, and the country has a long and storied history in international competition, but women were not allowed to wrestle or even allowed to watch wrestling in person.

Roshanzamir and her father have always been very close, and he helped her develop an interest in the sport from a young age — their living room became a makeshift wrestling room. "We would move the furniture out of the way and then we would wrestle on our Persian rug. I wrestled with my dad and then my mom would referee. He taught me a lot of takedowns. My dad also loved the cradle and he loved leg laces. We just had fun with it. We never thought me wrestling competitively was ever going to be a possibility."

Roshanzamir's father earned two PhDs, one in sociology and one in economics. When Roshanzamir was two years old, she moved with her family from Iran to Germany, where they stayed for four years. The family then lived in Austria for a year. They were away from Iran while her father pursued his degrees.

Coincidentally, Ziegler lived in Tehran, Iran for a year from 1978-79.

Marie Ziegler and Afsoon Roshanzamir — best of friends and teammates.

and the camp was being held in her hometown of Concord.

"I had never even been to a practice when I competed in that tournament and made my first World team," said Ziegler. "I accepted the challenge and gave it a try. I had watched a lot of wrestling when I was in high school and I loved the sport, but I had never wrestled until that day."

They obviously had no idea at the time, but Ziegler would eventually become Roshanzamir's training partner, teammate and best friend.

Roshanzamir advanced to the bronze-medal match in 1989 at the first World Championships in which the U.S. women competed. She stood

Her father was working over there and Ziegler attended third grade in the country. "It was pretty ironic that we had both lived in Iran. I really got a good dose of Iranian culture when I was there, and that was kind of a bond that Afsoon and I shared. Luckily, we got out of there."

Right around the time Ziegler and her family were leaving Iran, Roshanzamir and her family were moving back to Tehran. "It was a horrible time," said Roshanzamir. "About six months after we moved back to Iran, all hell broke loose. They had the revolution and the hostage crisis. Iran also went to war with Iraq."

Then came the news that sent shockwaves around the world. More than 60 American diplomats and citizens were taken hostage on November 4, 1979 after a group of Iranian revolutionary students took over the U.S. Embassy in Tehran. The Americans were held hostage for 444 days until their release on January 20, 1981.

"We quickly realized after we went back to Iran in 1979, 'Oh my God. We need to get the hell out of here,'" said Roshanzamir. "But it ended up taking us five years before we finally got out."

When she returned to Iran in 1979, at age seven, Roshanzamir had to learn the Persian language of Farsi. She had been speaking German because she had been going to a school in that country.

With the war going on with Iraq, her family experienced their share of traumatic moments. "When I was eight years old, I remember being on roller skates in my grandparents' backyard. I had a broomstick in my hand and I was trying to paddle as I skated. A bomb exploded near us and it shook the ground so hard that it knocked me off my skates. I remember falling right on my back. I looked up in the sky and I could see fighter jet planes and more bombs being dropped. After I got up, my grandma came out of the house and was yelling, 'Run, run' and I was trying to run with roller skates on.

"We were trying to run to get to shelter in a basement. I don't really remember what my emotions were, maybe because it was all just so surreal."

She recalled going to school, and seeing students missing from her classes. "I found out that their houses had been bombed and they had died. I have very vivid images of that."

Many nights, the family would be sitting at home when a red alarm would go off on their television. "It was to alert us that Iraqi planes were coming. So we would grab the flashlight and run down into the basement. You would hear the bombs going off, usually for two or three hours, and then we would eventually go upstairs when it stopped.

Wrestle Like A Girl

The 1980s represented the earliest days of women's wrestling in the U.S. Marie Ziegler

"We put duct tape, or whatever tape we could find, on the windows, in the form of an X, so they wouldn't shatter. And we would put blankets up inside the windows in case the windows did break."

The war between Iran and Iraq lasted for five years from 1979-84. "I was right in the midst of it the entire time."

Roshanzamir attended a German-Persian school in Iran in first and second grade. The school closed when she was in third grade because they didn't want Western influences when Islamic rule took over. "By the time I was in third grade, we were all covered up. Scarves were worn by all of the women. Islamic law has women covered up so no other man sees them. Women are considered men's possessions under Muslim law. Before Ayatollah Khomeini took over in 1979, Iran was very Westernized. Women wore mini-skirts and were into fashion. We watched American television shows. I remember watching the Bugs Bunny and the Woody Woodpecker cartoons. All of a sudden, all of that was gone. It became the Islamic Republic. There was no separation of religion and state. It was all one. Religious law became the law of the land.

"My family, we were not Muslim. I didn't believe in it and my family didn't believe in it, but we had to cover up because it was the law. There was no religious freedom under Islamic rule. We were forced to practice the Muslim religion. We had to pray in school, whether we liked it or not."

When school started in the morning, students at her all-girls school would line up by classes. "You would stand in these lines like they do in the United States for the Pledge of Allegianc. They would have us make a fist with our hands and do a chant every morning. They would make us chant, 'Marg bar Amrika,' which means "Death to the United States."

It was an anti-American political slogan that started when Ayatollah Khomeni came into power. "Every day we went to school and had to say, 'Death to the United States' 10 times. 'Death to England' 10 times and 'Death to France' 10 times. They would have flags of those countries on the ground at our schools. We had to stomp on the flags, and we stomped on American flags. I remember seeing American flags being burned."

Roshanzamir said the 2012 movie *Argo*, which won the Academy Award for Best Picture, offered a realistic view of what Iran was like in 1979. The movie chronicled the covert operation to rescue six Americans, which unfolded behind the scenes of the Iran hostage crisis. "There was a guy being hanged from a crane in the movie. I vividly remember seeing someone hanged from a crane when I lived in Iran. They wanted to make sure people knew what consequences they would face if they didn't obey the government."

Her parents eventually devised a plan for their family to leave Iran in 1984. "We told Iranian officials that my mom and I were going to Germany to visit relatives for one week. The government officials held onto our bank account, our house and my dad as collateral to make sure we went back to Iran, but we weren't going back. We left for Germany and never returned. My parents were planning for us to leave Iran, but they didn't tell me until a week before we left that we were moving to the United States. They said the United States was the land of freedom and opportunity. Right after that, I had a dream about the United States and that all of the streets there were made of gold."

Her father went into hiding after she fled to Germany with her mother in 1984. "My dad actually became his brother. My uncle, Fereydoun, was a German citizen. He had married a German woman. My dad got my uncle's German passport and took on his identity. They put my dad's photo on top of my uncle's photo in the passport, and tried to make it look authentic. My father had to make sure he had all of his brother's information from his passport memorized when he went to the airport on his way to Germany. My uncle is a lot taller than my dad, so my dad wore boots with big heels to make him look taller. We were all waiting for the phone call that he had made it to Germany. I remember my dad telling me his heart was beating really fast at the airport because he was so nervous before they checked his passport. My dad was finally able to get out of Iran three months after my mom and I left.

"I was 11 years old. I remember getting the call that my dad had made it to Germany, and it was such an anticipated moment. I remember we were cheering and celebrating because we were so excited to hear the news that he had made it out of Iran. If my dad had gotten caught, he probably would've been hanging from one of those cranes in Tehran like they showed in *Argo*."

Roshanzamir and her mother, Jila, went to San Jose, California, after leaving Iran and before her father was able to join them. Her mother had two sisters who had been living in the U.S. long before the revolution. "It was a very difficult time, but I love my life and I wouldn't change any part of it. That was just a part of it. Those experiences made me the person that I am today."

Being separated from her father was very stressful. "My dad gave me a stuffed animal, a rabbit, right before I left Iran for Germany with my mother in 1984. I held onto that stuffed animal, and that symbolized my dad when we were apart. I took that stuffed animal everywhere. It had a gold heart pendant stuffed inside it. I named it Rabbity. That stuffed animal held a lot of significance for me."

She has never returned to Iran since leaving in 1984. "I would love to go back, but I'm not sure how safe it would be for me, even after all these years. Iran was a great country with amazing people and an amazing culture before the revolution. It has been changed into violence and hatred. It's really sad to see. It is nothing of the beauty it had. I am Iranian-born but I can't relate to Iran anymore. What I like to remember is what it was like before the revolution when the country was Westernized and there were more freedoms. The country was very progressive and in a good state financially, but it was a monarchy.

"A lot of people thought they would have a better life after the revolution, but that hasn't been the case. It ended up being a lot worse because people have no freedom. They used to have freedom of religion and freedom of speech. There is lot more poverty and corruption and economic instability now. It breaks my heart."

She was excited about coming to America, but the transition was challenging. "My first six months in the U.S. were probably the hardest of my life. I didn't speak a word of English when I came to this country in 1984. My world had been turned upside down. I didn't have my dad there I and didn't know if I would ever see him again. We were in a new country and we didn't have money. We were well off in Iran, but we weren't able to bring any of that money with us to the U.S. My mom had to buy me clothes from garage sales. My favorite shirt I wore, my mom paid 10 cents for it at a garage sale. It was a white shirt with horizontal stripes that were pink and gold. It was a fuzzy sweater shirt."

Roshanzamir was 12 years old when she started school in her new country. "I was in sixth grade, and the kids were just brutal to me. They teased me and made fun of me. They would ask what nationality I was and I would say, 'Iranian.' That was like the worst word you could say to an American, especially right after the hostage crisis in Iran. That was another big strike against me. We had no money and we were poor. I carried my PE clothes to school in a plastic Kmart bag. It was very hard to get adjusted to the culture. Boys and girls didn't interact in Iran because it was segregated. I went to an all-girls school in Iran. So coming to the U.S., I was in school with boys and girls for the first time.

"I was pretty much blackballed at

At a 2013 wrestling reunion, Afsoon Roshanzamir met up with Joe Corso, her World team coach in 1989-90. Larry Slater

my school in the beginning. Nobody would talk with me and nobody would play with me. I was always very good at sports and I was very athletic. When it came time to play sports, I was the first one picked because I was a good athlete. That gravitated me toward being accepted more with my peers. I scored the winning point for our school's volleyball team in seventh grade and they did a story on me in the school newspaper. That helped me start to gain acceptance.

"I was eager to learn and I caught on very quickly. It only took me two months to learn English. I was already being considered for honors classes after that. I knew about survival, from what I had already been through in Iran, and I made adjustments quickly after coming to the U.S."

Afsoon received a fresh start when she started attending Independence High School in San Jose, California. That's where she met Marco Sanchez, who wrestled for Puerto Rico in the 1996 Olympic Games. "Marco was two years older than me, and my friend had a crush on him. I was a freshman in high school and Marco said something to her and I said, 'Hey, leave her alone.' He was standing there with his legs spread, shoulder-width apart, and he was facing me, but he was relaxed. I'm not sure why I did it, but I blasted him with a double-leg and he went right to his back in front of all of the wrestlers. He was the stud on the wrestling team."

Sanchez's eyes widened as he looked up at Roshanzamir: "You should go out for wrestling."

"Maybe I will," she fired back.

That night, when she arrived home from school, Roshanzamir approached her father: "Dad, I want to wrestle."

"That would be great," he responded.

"It wasn't quite the reaction you would expect from a father, but wrestling was something that always bonded us. I wasn't even thinking about wrestling when I first started high school. I had no designs to compete because I didn't fathom wrestling being a possibility for a girl at that time. That changed the day I double-legged Marco."

The next challenge came in convincing Independence coach David Chaid, father of NCAA champion Dan Chaid, that a girl should be allowed to compete in wrestling.

She approached Coach Chaid the next day: "I want to join the wrestling team."

"No way," Coach Chaid fired back. "This is a boys' team. You're going to get hurt."

Chaid didn't completely close the door on Afsoon. "But because of Title IX, you can wrestle if you want to," he said. "I can't stop you."

"Independence had a powerhouse program and the last thing he probably wanted was a girl on his wrestling team," said Roshanzamir. "Coach Chaid called my dad and my dad said it was okay for me to wrestle. I never quit because everyone expected me to. I had to be the only one who believed I wasn't going to be quitting. Nobody said anything to me, positively or negatively, when I first started."

She started wrestling competitively during the freestyle season the summer after her freshman season of high school. She lost every match, though she led 4-2 in what turned out to be her last match of the season. "The boy I was wrestling against panicked because he was losing to a girl. He did a full nelson, which is illegal, and picked me up and slammed me down onto the mat. My right collarbone snapped. We stopped at home before I went to the hospital. It was Mother's Day and I remember telling my mom, 'Happy Mother's Day. Where's my insurance card?'

"I remember everybody was probably thinking, 'There goes the end of her wrestling career.' They thought, 'Well, she won't be back.' I was determined to come back as soon as I could. I trained really hard with my dad that summer and worked my butt off."

She came back and won the first match of her sophomore season by a 17-2 technical fall. Wrestling against boys, she had a winning record that season. "The other guys on the team began looking at me as their little sister."

Dan Chaid, the son of Roshanzamir's high school coach, was close friends with Olympic and World champion Dave Schultz, and Chaid and Schultz would train at Independence High School on occasion. "Dave Schultz taught me my leg lace."

Among the boys she trained with was an up-and-coming eighth-grader named Eric Guerrero. Roshanzamir was a few years older, but she and Guerrero were the same size. "I would kick his butt and he would get so pissed off he would throw his headgear and storm out of the room."

Guerrero went on to wrestle for Independence High School before winning three NCAA titles for Oklahoma State and making the 2004 U.S. Olympic team.

Shortly after that, Roshanzamir made her first World team in women's freestyle wrestling in 1989. She wrestled in an international event at San Francisco State that served as the qualifier for the 1989 World team.

She lost to Japan's Miyu Yamamoto in the finals after beating her in an exhibition match the day before. Yamamoto went on to become a three-time World champion.

Roshanzamir had qualified for the 1989 World Championships, but there was another obstacle to overcome. "Those were the days before USA Wrestling funded the women at the Worlds. I had to pay all of my own travel expenses to compete. I went door-to-door asking people to donate money so I could wrestle in Switzerland. I raised what I could, and my parents paid the rest of it.

"I went to some businesses to raise money. I had a flyer made out with a picture of me in a wrestling jacket. Some businesses gave me $10 and some gave me $100. I got some good positive feedback and encouragement from a lot of them. Most of the people didn't know women wrestled back then, but people were pretty supportive when I told them about it. In those days, wrestling was a privilege not a right. We were just happy to be in the room and have a piece of the mat."

She started training at the 1989 World Team Camp, which is when she met Ziegler. "Marie was there with her boyfriend and I was there with my dad. Marie and I were warming up, just the two of us. I had a lot more of a wrestling background than Marie. I really pounded her that whole training camp. She would not give up. She took the beating, but just kept coming back and fighting. She was the toughest 100-pounder I had ever met. She didn't have technique then, but just had so much grit. She was so resilient. You couldn't break her. I slowly started gaining some respect and admiration for her. And we became great training partners for each other. She was very eager to learn, and she caught on very quickly."

Ziegler said she was determined to improve. "Afsoon kicked my butt every time. She had the boniest hips on the face of the Earth, and that made her very tough to score on. I definitely am stubborn. I had virtually no training or technique, but I watched a lot of wrestling when I was in high school and I loved the sport. I had heart and I wouldn't quit. I was persistent and just kept working at it. I learned a lot wrestling against Afsoon."

During those early days, the two girls also connected on a personal level. "Marie is like the sister I never had," said Roshanzamir. "It was just the two of us for a long time. We are very, very close. We could identify what each was going through. The bond that was created at that very first World team practice has never been broken. We were thrown into all of that together and that really bonded us. I would do anything for that girl, I really would.

"I absolutely love and adore Marie. She is one of the people in the world I most respect."

The feeling is mutual.

"We have a very special connection," said Ziegler. "She is like a sister to me. We are very, very close and have very complimentary personalities. She was a mentor for me on the mat, because she was more experienced, but I was kind of a mentor for her off the mat. I was 18 and she was 16 when we first met, and it was the first time she had really been away from her parents."

The bond was needed as female pioneers tried to prove they belonged.

"We encountered a lot of comments like, 'Oh my god, there's a girl wrestling.' It was kind of a freak show at times," said Ziegler. "It was a stigma we had to try and overcome. Some people were supportive, but a lot of people were very skeptical and critical of us."

Rusty Davidson guided the girls through some of those rough waters.

"Rusty was amazing," Ziegler said. "He had the perfect personality to coach us. He was extremely patient with us. He understood what we were up against and he taught us so much."

Roshanzamir made history by winning a bronze medal at the 1989 World Championships, just eight days after celebrating her 17th birthday. She lost to eventual runner-up Tomoku Natsumeda of Japan 4-3, then defeated Sandra Schumaker of Switzerland by injury default to earn bronze at 47 kilograms/103.5 pounds. "I threw the

Japanese girl with a nice head and arm throw, but it was right after time ran out."

Less than five years after leaving Iran, Roshanzamir had become the first American woman to win a World medal in international wrestling. Two of her teammates went on to earn World silver medals in 1989 — Asia DeWeese at 50 kilograms/110 pounds and Leia Kawaii at 70 kilograms/154 pounds. "I didn't totally understand the historical significance of what I had done at the time. I was still a teenager and still in high school. What I did know was that the United States really is the land of opportunity. There is nothing that can stop you except yourself and I was able to follow my dreams and become the first World medalist for the U.S. in women's wrestling.

"It meant a lot for me to have that opportunity. It was almost like a privilege. If I would've tried to wrestle for Iran, I would've been stoned or thrown in jail for doing that. Women weren't even allowed to go watch wrestling in Iran. I was very fortunate. I know there are a lot of women in Iran who would've loved to wrestle or have a chance to go watch wrestling in person."

Her trip to the 1989 Worlds added another dynamic since the men's freestyle and Greco-Roman teams in Iran were also competing there alongside the women. "I was told my name was on a blacklist in Iran because I wrestled and women from Iran aren't supposed to be wrestling. When I wrestled at the Worlds in 1989, all the Iranian men got up and left the arena when the women wrestled. I went up to shake the hand of an Iranian men's freestyle coach, and he said, 'I know who you are and I think that it's great that you wrestle. I'm sorry I can't shake your hand. There's eyes on us.'

"Some of the Iranian men's wrestlers walked by me and said, 'It's great that you wrestle' but refused to make eye contact with me because they were afraid they would get in trouble if someone saw them do that."

She came back to win a World silver medal in 1990, placing second behind Sweden's Asa Helena Pedersen at 47 kilograms. She advanced to the finals by knocking off returning World champion from Chinese Taipei, Yu Hsin Huang, in the semifinals. "I was behind in the semis and came back and tied the match 7-7. The match went into sudden-death overtime. There was no time limit, you just wrestled until someone scored. The match went on forever — it was crazy — and lasted close to eight minutes. We were both so exhausted. I spun behind her to get the winning takedown. I got up and raised my arms in celebration."

Roshanzamir said she was "still beyond exhausted" when she wrestled in the finals. "But I had wrestled the girl from Sweden a number of times and I had teched her every time. I was thinking before the finals that I was going to be a World champion. We came out for the finals and we were both wearing the wrong singlet colors. I first came out in red and my opponent was in blue. We had to go back and change singlets.

"I threw her in an arm spin for three points and she reversed me for two points. I thought all I had to do was hold the lead. Joe Corso was in my corner coaching me and he was yelling late in the match, 'Shoot, Afsoon, shoot.' I didn't shoot because I thought I was ahead 3-2. Time ran out and I was like, 'Yes, I won the World championship.' I thought I won, but then they raised my opponent's hand. I couldn't believe it. I still thought I was in red and it showed three points for red on the scoreboard. I looked down at the end of the match and I was wearing blue. We had switched singlet colors before the match. It was almost embarrassing for that to happen. There was no video review back then.

"I was shocked, absolutely just shocked and devastated. That was the single worst moment in my life. I didn't get beat. I lost it. She wasn't as good as me. I've thought about this a lot. I would have been the first U.S. World champion in women's wrestling.

"I stayed in the sport after that because I was going to keep chasing that gold medal. I still think about the match, though I try not to because it's so painful. The hardest part is it was my own mistake."

During the awards ceremony, she encountered another unhappy experience. "They gave out kitchen appliances because it was a women's-only Worlds in 1990. They gave me a sautée pan. Marie got a food processor. I thought it was very discriminatory toward the women. It just shows how far back we were. They had that mentality back then. They didn't give the outstanding wrestler award. Instead, they gave the prettiest wrestler award. Can you believe that? That's crazy. Even at that time, in 1990, we were pretty upset and very offended. We felt like we were making progress, but then you get knocked down a few notches when something like that happens. We were women wrestlers and trying to make a name for ourselves, but they were still thinking women should be pretty and be in the kitchen cooking."

Nevertheless, she had become the first two-time World medalist for the U.S. "My father was so proud. I don't think he ever expected to have his child make the World Championships because he didn't have a son to follow in his footsteps. He never thought I would have this opportunity. But we moved to America — the land of opportunity."

With Ziegler as maid of honor, Roshanzamir married Byron Johnston in 1998. Two years later, she retired. Her first of three children, a son, Aidan, was born in 2002.

"I just missed having a chance to wrestling in the Olympics when it debuted in Olympic competition for the women in 2004. The IOC voted in 2001 to add women's wrestling to the Olympic Games and it debuted in Athens, Greece, in 2004."

She was nine months pregnant with her daughter, Samira, during the 2004 Olympic Games. "I call her my Olympic gold medal. I watched Patricia Miranda win a medal for the U.S. at the 2004 Olympics. Miranda had never beaten me. I had beaten her three times. For her to get the first Olympic medal for the U.S., it was bittersweet. It was sweet that women's wrestling was in the Olympics and that the USA won a medal. I was already emotional being pregnant, and to not be able to compete in the Olympics was very difficult for me. I would've loved to have been out there. That was my dream. It wasn't easy for me to watch a girl I had defeated become the first U.S. woman to win an Olympic medal."

Her third child, a daughter, Layla, was born in 2005. "They would be good at it, but none of my kids wrestle. All three kids play soccer at the highest level for their age."

"What makes Afsoon so successful is she doesn't hold herself back," said Ziegler. "She always thought the sky was the limit, no matter what she was doing. It's magnificent to see how much positive energy she has. I love her perseverance. She will always find a way to get things done. She believed anything was possible. That had a huge impact on me."

Roshanzamir was named an Olympic coach for Team USA in 2016. "I never dreamed women's wrestling would come this far. To see how far it has come in a very short time, after what a lot of us went through in the early days, is just unbelievable. I am very proud and very honored to say that I was a part of this."

Ziegler captured World silver medals for the U.S. in 1990 and 1991 and later became the mother of two daughters, Mia and McKenna, and a son, McCartney. She returned to competition last year and won a Veterans World title in Greece.

Ziegler said the group of women's pioneers developed a tight bond that still exists. "We all had different personalities, but all the adversity and all the doubters made us strong as a core group. We had such a strong loyalty and allegiance to each other because we went through a lot of the same challenges when women first started wrestling. It was our job to open the door for women's wrestling, and for the girls who wrestle now it's their job to walk through. I never understood all of those people who were opposed to women's wrestling. A lot of those people would talk about wanting to grow the sport, but they didn't think women should wrestle.

"Fifty percent of the population is female. What better way to grow the sport of wrestling than to allow women to participate — it always made perfect sense to me."

CHAPTER 3
Tricia Saunders

Before Zeke Jones became a World champion and Olympic silver medalist, he lined up across the mat from an ambitious and determined young wrestler named Patricia McNaughton. And she didn't back down.

An eight-year-old weighing all of 50 pounds, McNaughton made an immediate impact on the mat. She wrestled in a club in Ann Arbor, Michigan run by Olympian and Michigan graduate Mark Johnson. In her first tournament, wrestling only against boys, she won seven out of nine matches. By the time she was 12, McNaughton had amassed a remarkable record of 181-23.

Among her victims was Jones, who went on to become one of the top men's freestyle lightweight wrestlers in American history. Jones later became USA Wrestling's National Freestyle Coach and he is now the head coach at Arizona State, his alma mater. "Growing up in Ann Arbor, Zeke lived just down the street from us. We were neighbors. He was born the same year that I was, but he was a year behind me in school since he didn't make the date cut-off. He hung out with my younger brother, Andy, who was a year younger. We'd go to wrestling practices and tournaments together — my dad would usually drive and we'd pick him up in our station wagon on the way.

"He was more like a younger brother to me. We'd practice together all the time and then compete against each other in tournaments. We were around the same weight, sometimes off one weight class but in the same age group. We had a bunch of really hard-fought matches and practices. Like normal kids, we'd also fight on the sidelines at times. He's always been like part of the

Tricia Saunders (far right) with a group of U.S. female wrestlers. USA Wrestling

family since we were little. There were times when we'd want to knock each other's block off — just like many brothers and sisters do. "

She said she won "most of the time" when she faced Jones in competition. "I remember him beating me once — he says it was twice," she said in 2016. "I don't remember exactly how many times I beat him — it was around 10-12 times that I won against Zeke. When we talk about it now, and I tell him he beat me just one time, it gets him real mad."

McNaughton was born on February 21, 1966 in Ann Arbor. Her mother's father, Al Steinke, was a football player who won a Big Ten wrestling title for the University of Michigan. Her own father, Jim, also wrestled at Michigan, as did her older brother, Jamie, before his career was cut short by an injury.

Jim McNaughton was a youth coach, and his two sons received an opportunity to wrestle at an early age. "I wondered why they got to wrestle, but not me," said McNaughton. "When my younger brother, Andy, started wrestling I could beat him up, so I knew I wanted to wrestle."

At age seven, while accompanying her brothers to practice, McNaughton made an announcement — she was bored with watching.

"Do you want to wrestle?" her father asked.

"Yes!" she replied emphatically.

When she was nine, she challenged the Amateur Athletic Union's ban on female participation in contact sports after she was told she was ineligible to compete in the association's national tournament because of her gender. She already had a 38-8 record competing against boys in wrestling by that time.

AAU guidelines prohibited females from participating in wrestling and boxing, but U.S. District Court Judge John Feikens ruled in June of 1975 that tournament officials must let McNaughton wrestle or not be able to hold the event. "States must take a leadership role in stamping out the denials of equal protection wherever the occur," the judge said.

By the time she was 12, McNaughton had become a dominant force in the youth wrestling ranks. She wanted to compete scholastically as she was about to enter seventh grade.

The Ann Arbor School Board met, and determined that she would not be allowed to wrestle at the junior high or high school levels. "When they kicked me out, I did gymnastics. I was decent in gymnastics, but I was a better wrestler than a gymnast."

McNaughton went on to earn her degree at the University of Wisconsin. Shortly after she graduated from college, Zeke Jones returned home from the 1989 World Championships and they ran into each other.

"Hey, they have women's wrestling in the World Championships now," Jones told her. "You should come back into the sport."

After a decade away from competition, she decided to give wrestling another shot. In 1989, she moved to Phoenix, Arizona, where a number of top male wrestlers were training with the Sunkist Kids Wrestling Club.

Sunkist Kids founder Art Martori and Arizona State coach Bobby Douglas had built a very strong club with numerous wrestlers who won Olympic and World titles. That success went hand-in-hand with what Arizona State was doing. The Sun Devils had won the 1988 NCAA team title with Jones and McNaughton's brother, Andy, on that championship squad.

"Sunkist was the number one freestyle team in the nation at the time," she said. "And Art Martori was the one most instrumental for getting the women's national movement up and going. I trained down there and started wrestling with the guys. I had Zeke down there, and they also had Marco Sanchez, Rob Eiter and Tim Vanni. All of those guys wrestled in the Olympics. They were particularly helpful because they were my size."

She made a quick transition back to wrestling. "I hadn't wrestled in 10 years. It was a giant learning curve for me because I hadn't competed for so long.

Tricia Saunders working for a turn on her opponent. USA Wrestling

But I was fortunate because I was surrounded by so many great lightweight wrestlers. If it weren't for Zeke's invitation to resurrect my interest in wrestling in Arizona, none of this wrestling stuff would ever have happened to me. Zeke really helped me a lot with my technique. He's a fantastic coach and a real fine technician. Anybody can learn a lot from that guy. It's kind of nice how all of that came around with Zeke after we grew up together in Michigan."

Among the standout wrestlers in the ASU room when McNaughton returned to wrestling was Dave Schultz. "Dave would show me stuff, and I would write it down and take it all in. I saw a lot of really good wrestlers from all over the world in that room. There were no other girls in the room although some came aboard a bit later."

Her first national tournament came in 1990. "I was a little nervous and I didn't know how it would go since I never had wrestled many of the American girls before, but I did win. I was the only Sunkist wrestler — other girls came in from various parts of the country."

In her first World Championship, in 1990 in Sweden, she suffered an injury late in her first-round match at 50 kilograms/110 pounds. She had dislocated a shoulder for the second time in three weeks and had to default. Major surgery followed. "Every doctor told me I was finished with wrestling. I had to decide if I wrestled because I liked to compete or because I liked to win."

McNaughton placed sixth in 1990 and fifth in 1991 in her first two World Championships. She came into the 1992 Worlds in Villeurbanne, France at the top of her game. Earlier that year, she had married standout ASU wrestler Townsend Saunders, who went on to a win an Olympic silver medal in 1996.

Now competing as Tricia Saunders, she opened the 1992 Worlds by pinning Aracely Jimenez of Venezuela in 26 seconds and Britt Solstad of Norway in 2:55. Her third bout was against two-time World champion Martine Poupon of France, who she beat 3-0.

In the gold medal finals, she beat Japan's Yoshiko Endo, a 1991 World silver medalist, 7-3. She was voted the tournament's best technical wrestler. And then there was the minor detail of becoming the first American woman to win a World wrestling title.

"That tournament was a real highlight. It was great having my husband as my coach in the corner. He really helped me. On one occasion during the finals I got hipped over for two points. I was still fighting it and I was getting into a position where I could have gone onto my back. But he yelled at me to 'let go' and I did, and I didn't give up any back points."

National coach Rusty Davidson was impressed with her performance. "Tricia did everything she trained for and what she expected to do. She is a real hero," Davidson said after the match. "She trained hard, made sacrifices and got what she went for. Tricia is in great physical condition, strong, clean technically, and was well-prepared."

The move to Arizona had paid huge dividends for Saunders. "It was really a career defining move to go out to Phoenix after graduating from college. My brother went to Arizona State. Zeke had recruited my brother and they wrestled for Bobby Douglas. I figured I would like Arizona — it was nice and warm and I could be with my brother. I started working and training out there at the same time. I was a micro-biologist. I had to work full-time while I was competing because there was no financial support for women, so that was different."

With women's wrestling virtually brand-new worldwide, Saunders dealt with her share of cynics and critics. "There was prejudice everywhere. It was surprising how many people — coaches, administrators, parents — could slam doors against giving opportunities for girls to wrestle. People were actually fighting to keep girls out of the sport."

Finding competition domestically was difficult for American girls in those early days for women who were wrestling in the United States. "I'd have to go oversees and compete internationally to get matches some of the time. To

Tricia Saunders accepts USA Wrestling Women's Wrestler of the Year award from Jim Scherr. USA Wrestling

go over to Europe was not a big deal — there would be hundreds of girls wrestling in tournaments."

Japan had taken the lead as the dominant country in women's wrestling, and remains on top in the world at the highest level. "They had girls wrestling in colleges. When I was there in the 1990s, wrestling was just like another extension of a martial art. In 1991, I'd go wrestle a Japanese girl who was 18 years old, but she has been competing since she was five. There would be cameras following the Japanese wrestlers around the city because they were famous, and then I come back to the U.S. 48 hours later where girls and women are told they can't wrestle and that it is not even a sport.

"People back here were not really interested in your wrestling story. People back here were not very brave. There were a few who stood out to defend women's wrestling, but they took a lot of heat for it and that is really too bad. When I was growing up, there was no girls' soccer or girls' softball, but those sports advanced quickly because people were ready to invest in the sport. That was not true for women's wrestling. Wrestling leaders early on failed in the U.S. to support the sport."

Saunders said it was a source of huge frustration for the women. "It was in 1990 or 1991 when USA Wrestling declared that they would not support women's wrestling: they only would say that they would not stand in our way. They said, 'We won't allow women to compete at USA Nationals because it will degrade the integrity of the tournament.' They didn't want to have to see girls wrestling against girls.

"You are talking about intelligent people who love the sport, who are real nice to you, who walk around and then slam the doors. I was on the USA Wrestling board for the first time in 1992. There was no one else on the board who wanted to help women's wrestling except Art Martori. When I went and spoke to the board after winning the World Championship in 1992, they changed their mind except for one former president of USA Wrestling, who voted against.

"I was on the board because of Martori. They needed a women's athlete representative for the Women's Advisory Committee so I was appointed. In their 30-plus years of existence, USA Wrestling has elected just one woman to the board — Nancy Schultz — in an At-Large capacity. It has always just been someone appointed to a position that had to be filled by a woman. It is much the same at the state level as well. Yes, things have changed a lot in the last 25 years for women's wrestling equality, but it has a very long way to go. You look at the national governing bodies of gymnastics or track and field and it is clearly

Tricia Saunders is outspoken about the gender inequality still found in wrestling circles. Larry Slater

not the same."

Saunders' style of wrestling was constantly evolving. "I specialized in the overhook series. I used the high crotch a lot as well. I learned and used throws as well, having it as a threat a lot of times like the judo wrestlers. Since girls don't sweat like guys, you will see a lot more throws in the women's matches because the guys are so sweaty they can't hang onto their opponents.

"Later on, Steve Fraser helped me with a side headlock from several different positions which I ended up using from time to time. Bobby Douglas helped me to use three different attacks, moving forward and then, depending upon what your opponent does next, you make one of three different moves. I could usually count on my inside trip or one of my arm spins to score points. I liked to wrestle a lot more from the tie than from the outside."

Saunders advanced to the World finals for the second straight year in 1993 before falling to eventual five-time World champion Xiue Zhong of China in the gold-medal match. "Since I was the defending champion, people were expecting me to win, but I didn't consider myself the favorite because she had more World medals than me.

"She was better than me that day. I just didn't wrestle very well. When I did score it was a 2-2 move since she initiated the action. I did come back to beat her at the World Championships in 1999, which was the only other time I wrestled her. She was the best girl I ever wrestled. She was really tough."

Saunders placed fourth at the 1995 Worlds before capturing three more World titles in 1996, 1998 and 1999.

When Saunders won her fourth World title in 1999, teammate Sandra Bacher also captured a gold after earning silver and bronze medals the previous two years.

Shannon Williams also excelled in the 1990s, reaching the finals of the World Championships on four occasions. Williams finished a stellar career as a four-time World silver medalist for the U.S.

Saunders completed her Hall of Fame career with five World medals — four gold and one silver. "I was ready to retire after winning the Worlds in 1999. I was 33 years old, but then I thought that I might wrestle in an exhibition match at the 2000 Olympic Games. Then we were hosting the 2001 Worlds in New York City. I had never competed in front of a large crowd in the USA, so I said, 'Okay, maybe I'll do this one more time. But then the World Trade Center came down and I said, 'That's it.'"

The 2001 World Championships were moved to Bulgaria, and that turned out to be the last World-level event in which Saunders competed. She never had the chance to wrestle in the Olympic Games, but she was one of the coaches of the first U.S. Women's Olympic Wrestling Team, at the 2004 Games. She coached alongside her husband, Townsend, and national coach Terry Steiner when women's wrestling made its Olympic debut.

Saunders has been inducted into the National Wrestling Hall of Fame and the United World Wrestling International Hall of Fame while remaining active in wrestling on the USA Wrestling Board of Directors.

She and her husband have three children — two daughters, Tassia and Tatiana, and a son, Townsend.

Saunders played a huge role in putting women's wrestling on the map during a time where they faced more than their share of obstacles. "I'm proud to have been a part of that. There was a lot of adversity that we had to overcome."

But she admits to being disappointed that the sport hasn't grown more now that women's wrestling is in the Olympic Games. "In the U.S., wrestling has really not kept up with the times as far as development of the sport compared to other Olympic women's sports. I find wrestling people always talk among themselves and compare what is happening today in wrestling with the past. That is how they measure progress. I tell them that they have to stop comparing to 10 years ago.

"We have to compare ourselves to other sports — today's soccer, for instance, or today's track and field. And we know that wrestling is way, way behind the eight-ball. In the junior high and senior high schools, girls still have to try out for the school team against the boys. That's not the case in the other Olympic sports like soccer, softball and gymnastics."

Wrestle Like A Girl

CHAPTER 4
Iris Smith

The summer after she finished eighth grade, Iris Smith showed up to watch her older brother practice freestyle wrestling with some of the other high-school athletes.

Born and raised in Albany, Georgia, she was the middle child of five in her African-American family. She had an older brother and older sister along with a younger brother and younger sister. In addition, there were two half-sisters and a half-brother included in the clan. Her mother was a cheerleader and her father played basketball; he was a career soldier in the U.S. Army and Air Force. "Sports were always a big thing in our family. My brothers were into football and wrestling. I had a sister who was into tennis and track. My other sister wrestled a little bit, but was more musically inclined."

During one of the freestyle practices Smith attended, the team's coach, Anthony White, a retired Marine, caught a glimpse of her trying a few wrestling moves with the boys.

"Hey, you look like you could have some potential as a wrestler," White said. "Why not come out for the team?"

"No, I can't do that," Smith responded politely. "This is a guys' sport."

Coach White then approached her parents and suggested she try out for the team. She eventually agreed to join in practicing with the boys, but during her second day of training she crumpled to the mat with an injury.

She had broken her ankle.

"That didn't get me down because I liked the sport and I came back. After I healed, I went back to wrestling during the school season. I made the B team in the 145-pound weight class. Eventually, I wrestled off for varsity and won several varsity matches. I lost some as well."

In addition, she was elected Student

Iris Smith is crowned 2005 World champion in Budapest. Larry Slater

Council President of her class at Darsey High School.

The following year, 1995, Smith entered her first U.S. Open and competed exclusively against women in that event. She finished fourth in her weight class. "There were all the big-time wrestlers there — World champions Tricia Saunders and Sandra Bacher. I was awed by them. I was good enough to start traveling with the Senior team. I went on a tour with USA Wrestling to Sweden and New Zealand. I was 16 at the time — there was no Junior team for the girls.

"I no longer was wrestling for my high school team since I wanted to concentrate on freestyle at the Senior women's level. I knew at that point that I wanted to be an Olympian. I wanted to win some medals. I was dedicated to doing that."

Smith said she didn't encounter much resistance to being a female wrestler, but she did recall one time in high school being approached by an administrator at her school. "My principal, who was a very nice guy, came up and said to me, 'Iris, do you know it's not proper for young ladies to wrestle?' But my mom and my family supported me all the way. I felt that wrestling was the sport where

I found success and that I was going to continue to compete. I didn't let any prejudice affect or bother me because I saw the bigger picture. I saw the U.S. World team members traveling around the world and knew that I could have a chance to do the same if I kept with it.

"I was also fortunate to have a wrestling coach who sought me out, who talked me into coming into the sport and was so supportive of me. And my older brother was a pretty good wrestler on the high school team. He would work out with me and gave me lots of support. My coach made sure that I was treated no differently than any of his other wrestlers."

She recalled that boys weren't all that crazy about losing to a girl. "I was competing at a freestyle tournament and my mom arrived a little bit late. When she came into the gym, there was this kid crying off to the side. He was all emotional and started running out the door. She stopped him to ask him if he was okay. He said, 'Not really. I just lost to a girl.' And my mom quickly figured out that I was the girl that he was talking about. That was one of my first big wins because he was actually pretty good."

In the summer of 1998 Smith had a big decision to make — go off to college to continue her wrestling career or take a leap of faith and move to Colorado Springs to train year-round at the Olympic Training Center (OTC). "After high school, I was considering going to college at Minnesota-Morris where they had one of the two college wrestling programs for women in the U.S. My mom analyzed the situation and suggested that I try the Olympic Training Center instead of college. I said 'fine', but I remember being sad. I loaded up the car and said goodbye to my family. My mom said, 'It's going to be fine, Iris. Pretend that it's just a long wrestling trip.' That made it so much better for me."

So Smith became just the second woman to train year-round at the OTC. "There was one girl who started about a year before me — Christy Jeffries from Florida. We were the first females training there. Kevin Jackson was the resident coach at the time. The women's program wasn't developed yet so I practiced with Kevin and his men. He was very welcoming in opening the room to us. I'd just show up for practices and do whatever was asked.

"I didn't have a place to live on campus. Christy and I rented a townhouse. We had to find jobs to support ourselves. I did receive a small stipend from USA Wrestling since I was on the national team. I found a job at a women's clothing store as a stylist and store clerk. I did that for several years and then became a security guard for Compaq Computers where I could choose the better hours to work in accordance with my training schedule. Finally, in 2001 I joined the Army and

Iris Smith was the first African-American woman to win a World championship. John Sachs

was accepted into the U.S. Army's World Class Athlete Program."

Smith won the U.S. Senior championships in 2000 and 2001 and placed seventh at the Worlds in 2000.

Five years later, she earned a berth in the 2005 Worlds in Budapest, Hungary. "It definitely helped that I had competed in the Worlds before — I had experienced it and I knew what to expect. I knew that I could wrestle with any of the girls in the weight class. I knew I could win a World title."

During the team's acclimation camp, in Prague, Czech Republic, Army coach Shon Lewis approached her just before the Worlds. "When you look in the mirror at the end of the day," Lewis told her, "you know if you've put in all of the hard work."

"I knew I had worked really hard," said Smith. "I prepared the right way and I was ready. I felt great and I felt confident. I wasn't one of the favorites and I think that motivated me, too."

She was in a loaded weight class at 72 kilograms/158.5 pounds that included Japanese legend Kyoko Hamaguchi and an eventual five-time World champion in Stanka Zlateva of Bulgaria. Smith downed Zlateva 3-1, 1-0 in the first round and added two more wins before advancing to the finals against Hamaguchi.

"I was in a zone. I was able to stay focused on each match. I was in a place where I knew I could do it."

She countered a move by Hamaguchi early in the match and caught the Japanese star on her back. "That was my first opportunity to wrestle her. I knew she was good, but I was coming out there to win that match. Everybody wants to beat a champion and that was my mindset. She came out very aggressively, but I was ready for the challenge. I wasn't intimidated by her."

Hamaguchi fought back, but Smith eventually earned a 3-1, 1-1, 1-0 victory in the gold-medal match. "I dug a little deeper to win that match. All the hard work I did paid off for me."

Smith raised her arms in victory and then placed her hands over her face. "I just kept saying to myself, 'Oh my God, oh my God.' I did this. I'm a World champion.'"

After her hand was raised in victory, Smith charged over to the corner and jumped into the arms of coaches Lewis and Terry Steiner. "I was so excited. It was an overwhelming feeling."

Smith said the medal ceremony was a memorable experience. "I wanted to hear our national anthem and see our flag raised. Being able to experience that while standing on top of the podium was incredible. Whenever I hear the national anthem now, it always takes me back to that day."

Steiner was impressed with the way his heavyweight performed on what turned out to be the biggest day of her career. "Iris was wrestling really well going into the Worlds. She trained that summer with a girl from Germany who had won European titles, and Iris was doing well against her. She came out very determined and wrestled a perfect tournament. She got hot at the right time. You got to perform when the stakes are highest and Iris was ready to go. It was fun to be a part of. She earned that World title."

In winning the World Championship in 2005, Smith became the first U.S. African-American World champion among women wrestlers. She was not the first African-American woman medalist, however. That honor belongs to Leia Kawaii, who won a silver in 1989 at the first World Championships the U.S. entered.

Smith also became a role model for one of the greatest U.S. women wrestlers — Adeline Gray. In a recent interview, Gray talked about the first time she met Smith. "When I was 15 [2006] I entered a boy's tournament in Fort Carson which is called the State Games. Iris Smith, the 2005 World champion, was there. She came to sign autographs. She is the biggest girly-girl, with her nails and hair all done up. She walks into practice looking glamorous; reminds me of Serena Williams — a beautiful African-American woman who carries herself with poise and grace. She walks in and shows us her medal from winning the Worlds. That was the first time that I remember looking at her and seeing someone who was both a successful woman and a wrestler.

"I just loved it. She signed my headgear and I remember thinking, 'Wow, I could be a World champion one day.'

"That was the first time that I had that type of dream and I saw a role model for myself. I met her and realized that, 'This is real and wrestling can take me somewhere'. I didn't do well in the tournament but recall this as a defining moment in my life. She was so beautiful and athletic."

Smith continued to excel well into her 30s as a member of the Army's World Class Athlete Program. She won a gold medal for the Army and the United States at the 2010 World Military Championships and made the U.S. World Team again in 2012.

"My Military World championship title in 2010 is one of the accomplishments that I am most proud of. There were just two Americans that won the gold medal — Dremiel Byers and myself. We were wrestling the best wrestlers in all the military forces around the world. Everyone was in their military uniforms when off the mat and it was such a pageant. Standing on the top of the platform and hearing the 'Stars and Stripes' being played in front of all these military personnel from around the world was a huge honor."

Smith made numerous U.S. national

teams and also competed at the 2012 and 2016 Olympic Trials.

Her only big regret was not winning an Olympic medal. At the 2016 trials, she joined Kristie Davis as one of the two veterans giving it their last shot of making an Olympic team. "I wanted to be an Olympian my whole competitive career. I felt good and thought I'd have a chance. Earlier in the year I had to injury default out of my matches — for the first time in my life — at the Pan Ams in Texas and I didn't want to go out that way. I went through an intensive rehab program preparing for the trials. I gave it my best effort but it was not quite enough."

Smith retired upon the completion of the trials, the end of a 22-year journey, including 17 years on the Senior level. "Unfortunately, I completely forgot about the tradition of taking off your shoes and leaving them on center mat."

Smith joined the Army coaching staff and continues to live in Colorado Springs. "Wrestling for the Army has been great — I have no regrets at all. I come from a big military family. The military was always an option, whether I was still wrestling or not. Being able to do a sport I love and be in the military, I was all in. The Army is more than just a team — we are a family. All of the wrestlers, we feed off each other. We are very supportive of one another.

"I'm so happy I decided to become a wrestler. When I first started, I missed my prom and graduation because of wrestling. I remember being on teams with Trish Saunders and Afsoon. I competed with and against Kristie Marano for years, and then [in 2015] I wrestled with Kristie's daughter at the Olympic Training Center.

"The sport of women's wrestling has progressed so much. We still have a long way to go, but there are a lot more opportunities for girls now. I want to stay involved in the sport. I learned the value of hard work, how to overcome adversity and what it's like to be on a close-knit team. I wouldn't trade that experience for anything."

Wrestle Like A Girl

CHAPTER 5
Kristie Marano

Kristie Marano was on top of the podium. And on top of the world. Competing in her home state and home country on the sport's biggest stage, Marano stepped onto the mat at New York City's historic Madison Square Garden and began to dominate her opponents.

Wrestling at the 2003 World Wrestling Championships, she breezed through four matches by fall, technical fall, fall and fall to storm into the women's freestyle finals at 67 kilograms/147.5 pounds. Already a World champion in 2000, she had advanced to an impressive sixth World final after placing second in her first four trips to the gold-medal round.

Backed by family, friends and a boisterous home American crowd, Marano won the 2003 World title with a 7-1 win over Poland's Ewelina Pruszko. She had won her second World title.

Marano smiled and waved to the crowd with both hands as she stood atop the podium as the USA flag was raised while the "Star-Spangled Banner" was played on American soil. She led the U.S. team to a first-place tie with Japan (Japan was declared the winning team by virtue of having more individual champions), and she was the lone American champion among a record seven USA medalists. "It was awesome, being able to win this not only in the USA, but in the state I grew up in, New York. It's like a dream come true. This was different because I am only an hour and 45 minutes from my home. Teamwise, we have done tremendously. This team is great. We have worked really hard and we deserve every medal we get."

She was also able to share the emotional victory with her young daugh-

Kristie Marano won nine World Championship medals. USAW

ter, Kayla. "My daughter enjoys it. She loves it," Marano said in 2003. "She's my number one fan."

The win in New York also gave her a huge boost of confidence and momentum going into 2004, the year that women's wrestling would make its debut at the Olympics. With just four weight classes, Marano had a choice to make in her quest to make the American team — drop down to 63 kilograms/138.75 pounds and battle 2003 World silver medalist Sara McMann, or bump up to 72 kilograms/158.5 pounds and challenge 2003 World silver medalist Toccara Montgomery.

She chose to cut down to 63 kilos and the move appeared to pay off when she pinned McMann in the 2004 U.S. Open finals in April. She would be the favorite to win the Olympic Trials and have an opportunity to be part of the historic first U.S. Olympic women's wrestling team that would compete in Athens.

She was born Kristie Stenglein on January 24, 1979, the first of three children — she has two younger brothers, Matt and Joshua. Her father, Conrad, worked doing inspections on military equipment and her mother, Nancy, was a dental hygienist assistant. Conrad Stenglein had wrestled in high school and later competed in judo.

She took up judo at the age of five, but also was around wrestling as her brothers started to compete in that sport. Her father coached her in judo and coached her brothers in wrestling. She wrestled in her first match at age 10, and her father was impressed. "Oh, I think you can do this," he said. "It's not much different than judo."

"Well, I went out there in the boys' tournament and did okay," she said. "Until I got a concussion."

She told her father, "That's it for wrestling. I'm not doing this anymore. I don't like it."

She excelled in judo, and competed in her first Senior-level tournament as a 13-year-old in Colorado Springs, finishing third. "My mom and dad went with me and we spent a bunch of money on airfare to get out there. When I went to check in for the tournament, the officials said to us, 'Sorry, you are too young to enter the tournament. Absolutely not, we have never had a 13-year-old in this tournament. This is for Seniors.' Some of the holds that the Seniors use, like arm bars and chokes, you are not permitted to do until you are a certain age. It was pretty crazy, but they ended up letting me compete."

Two years later, she made the U.S. Junior World team in judo, and was just 15 years old when she competed at the Junior World Championships in Cairo, Egypt.

She also played softball, making her

high school varsity team as a freshman, and basketball. "Even though I was only 5-foot-5, I was playing center on the basketball team. I weighed about 150 pounds and I was known for being tough and for not being afraid to get under the basket and fight for a rebound."

Her father put an end to the basketball career after her sophomore year at Colonie Central High School in Albany, New York. "I think this is ridiculous," Conrad told his daughter. "You are wasting your time with basketball and you have Olympic Trials [in judo] coming up next year. You have no future in basketball. You are 5-foot-5. I don't care what you do, but you are not playing basketball anymore."

Suddenly, she was looking for a new winter sport to play in school. She talked to one of the wrestlers on the team, who said, "You really ought to come out for wrestling."

"No, I'm not wearing a singlet," she responded. "And I'm not wearing one of those caps on my head. I'm not doing it."

Her father offered another suggestion: "You have two choices — you can go wrestle for the high school team or you can just do judo all the time."

In the fall of 1995, she and her father arranged a meeting with Colonie Central head wrestling coach Andy Monin. "Can Kristie come in and practice with the boys?" Conrad asked.

"No, you just can't come in to the practices," Coach Monin said. "You have to be part of the team — all or nothing."

The father looked at his daughter and said, "Go do it, Kristie. This is what you have to do."

Two weeks into wrestling season, she blew out her anterior cruciate ligament in her knee. With the 1996 Olympic Trials in judo scheduled for the next month, she elected not to have surgery. "Needless to say, the Olympic Trials did not go very well. I consider the ACL as the stabilizer for the knee. I remember at the trials going out there with my knee all taped up. It took just one foot-sweep, which knocked me out and I was done. Basically, I competed for the next five years just wearing a brace without getting my knee fixed."

She eventually made the varsity in wrestling at 145 pounds and finished with a .500 record. "That was a rugged weight class. The boys were now pretty much men — tough and strong. I had a unique situation, though, because of my background in judo, and most of the people in the area knew me or knew of me. They knew my brothers and how good they were. So by the time I came into wrestling, the people around the city knew who I was. I feel that if I wasn't already a known entity, if I was just another girl who came out and wanted to start wrestling, it would have been totally different. I was already accepted as an athlete, not as a girl, not just by my teammates but by the people around the Capital region.

"I never had a wrestler on the team who wouldn't work out with me. I always had one of the guys as a partner. I never had a male opponent refuse to wrestle me. The guys knew that I knew what I was doing on the mat, and unless they gave it their all, I was going to throw them. I was not your typical single-leg, double-leg wrestler. I used the throws that came naturally to me from judo. I was more like a Greco wrestler."

Wrestling against boys benefited her when she started facing girls on the national and international levels. "I had the mindset that I had worked hard while wrestling against boys. I was getting pushed and beat up by these boys, and in my mind, I was not going to let a girl beat me. I know that's what the boys say but that's okay for me to say because I'm a girl. I know I worked just as hard as these guys. These boys in my weight class were good — they went and placed at Fargo. I don't know where that mindset came from — maybe from my judo experience."

She started focusing more on wrestling and she made her first U.S. Senior World Team as a 17-year-old in 1996. "It was a whole new world for me. I didn't have any international experience, so I didn't know what to expect. But I thought I could do well because of my judo background."

She made an immediate splash, advancing to the gold-medal match at her first Senior World Championships in Sofia, Bulgaria. Her finals opponent was four-time World champion Dong Feng Liu of China. Marano dropped that match, but earned a World silver medal for the United States and followed with three more World silver medals from 1997-99. She fell to Japan's Kyoko Hamaguchi three straight times in the finals. (Hamaguchi finished her career as a five-time World champion.) But she did capture a Junior World wrestling title in 1998.

Her second-place finish in 1999 was key to the U.S. women's team winning their country's only World Championship title. "Those first four years at the World Championships, I remember getting pretty much crushed in the finals. I was like, 'Holy cow, I'm tired of finishing second.' I would beat myself up pretty bad about that. I shouldn't have, but that's the way I felt. I'm extremely hard on myself and I'm my own worst critic. I was not happy about finishing second four years in a row. That was rough."

She said she benefited from the influence and input from a number of women's wrestlers, including Tricia

Saunders and Shannon Williams. "The older girls were great. They took me under their wing. I was very young, and they gave me a lot of advice and encouragement. That made a big difference for me.

"What Trish did for women's wrestling was huge — she made so many great contributions to the sport. Not only was she a great wrestler, but she was also a great leader. She would always encourage me to work hard and not give up. She saw that potential in me. She had a lot of experience and she would tell me what to expect."

During her early run of World success, Marano gave birth to her daughter, Kayla, on April 15, 1998. "It was in 1998 and I went to Chicago for University Nationals. I was 19, and I suspected I was several months pregnant, though it turned out it was nearly nine months. I hadn't gained all that much weight. I still qualified my weight class, 138 pounds. I won the tournament and I flew back home."

Two weeks later, she awoke in pain. Her water had broken. "I was too ashamed to wake my parents — I hadn't told them about any of this. I went into the bathroom and delivered my six-pound, seven-ounce girl in the bathtub. After cutting the umbilical cord, I remember driving with her to the store to get diapers and formula. Later in the morning, I finally told my folks about the ordeal. They were shocked, but very supportive. My dad gave me a big hug."

Just 10 days later, with her doctor's approval, she won her third U.S. Senior women's title by defeating World medalist Sandra Bacher in the finals.

Seven more World medals, including two gold, would follow after Kayla was born. "I brought Kayla to practices and competitions all the time. She grew up around wrestling."

She married Kayla's father, but that marriage only lasted two years. She was no longer just a women's wrestling champion. She was a single mother.

Despite the added responsibilities of raising a daughter, Marano continued to excel on the mat. The big breakthrough came in 2000 after she dropped down to 68 kilograms/149.5 pounds. After four straight years of setbacks in the finals, she struck gold with a 6-5 overtime win over Russia's Anna Shamova in Sofia, Bulgaria.

As she walked off the mat, U.S. coach Mike Duroe met her in the corner. "Russia might protest the match," he said. "Make sure you stay ready."

"I had just wrestled my ass off and then they were saying I might have to wrestle another match in five minutes," said Marano. "I was not happy at all."

But the result of the match was upheld and Marano had become a World champion for the first time. "I was excited — it was overwhelming to win a World title."

Then came that second World title in 2003. "That's my most memorable experience as a wrestler. A lot of my family and friends had never seen me wrestle internationally. My grandpa was my biggest supporter and for him to see me wrestle was huge. Winning a World title in front of all of them, in New York, is something I will never forget. I had so much support from so many people. It was an awesome moment."

Now she was ready to land a spot on the U.S. team for the first Olympic Games for women's freestyle wrestling in 2004. But she first had to win a battle with the scale as she dropped down from the non-Olympic weight class of 67 kilograms/147.5 pounds to the Olympic weight class of 63 kilograms/138.75 pounds. She had cleared her first hurdle by winning the 2004 U.S. Open at 63 kilos — now there was the Olympic Trials.

She and Coach Terry Steiner boarded the same flight from Denver to Indianapolis for the 2004 Olympic Trials. "How's your weight?" Steiner asked.

"Two over," she said.

"Kristie was only two pounds over, but she was very dehydrated," Steiner said. "The next day was weigh-ins. I got out of a press conference around

Kristie Marano once again looks for the fall at the 2007 Worlds in Azerbaijan. Larry Slater

noon, and I saw that she was having difficulty taking off any more weight. It was like her body was shutting down and not letting go of any weight anymore. So, the rest of that afternoon we were in and out of the sauna, and she was really breaking mentally. Not that

she was fighting it, it was just that she didn't have anything left."

The last of the weight didn't come off — Marano was unable to make 63 kilograms. "I went from the biggest high of my life in 2003 to the crappiest year of my life in 2004 from a wrestling standpoint. I was caught in between weight classes, and 63 kilos was a huge cut for me. It just wasn't a natural weight class for me. It hurt for a long time. I can't blame anybody but myself. You just have to regroup and move on."

But she had another option to try

and make the 2004 Olympic team — moving up to 72 kilograms/158.5 pounds. She battled tough, like she always did, in the best-of-three finals against Toccara Montgomery. She lost in overtime in the first match and by one point in the second match.

"Toccara was second in the World the year before, but Kristie was holding her own in those matches," Steiner said. "She was ahead in one of the matches with just seconds left but got beat. In losing, yes, she was very disappointed but she handled things right. She will always go down as one of the very best competitors I have ever been around. You could always count on Kristie to give everything she had when she stepped out there to wrestle."

Montgomery was headed to Athens, while Marano, a two-time World champion and six-time World finalist at that point, fell short of making the first U.S. Olympic team in women's wrestling.

"That was a bone-crusher right there," Marano said in 2012. "It's just heartbreaking. There's just no other way to put it. My goals and my dreams were to make it to the Olympics."

She returned to the World stage in 2006 in Guangzhou, China. Back up to her heavyweight class at 72 kilograms/158.5 pounds, she won bronze, her eighth career World medal.

The next year, in Baku, Azerbaijan, she made a record seventh World final, qualifying the U.S. for the 2008 Olympics at 72 kilograms. In the semifinals, Marano battled 2004 Olympic silver medalist Guzel Manurova of Russia. Manurova shot in on a leg attack and Marano countered aggressively, launching the Russian to her back to record a quick and stunning 49-second fall.

As Marano walked off the mat, she was overcome by emotion. She held her hand over her face as tears streamed down her cheeks.

Not known for doing a lot of scouting of her opponents, she was informed right after the match that she had just beaten an Olympic silver medalist. "Oh, that's cool. I didn't know that."

Marano had clinched an American record ninth World medal, tying her with Bruce Baumgartner for the most World medals won by an American wrestler, regardless of gender. Not a bad accomplishment considering the women didn't wrestle in their first World Championships until 1989.

In the final, Marano fell to returning champion Stanka Zlateva of Bulgaria, going home with a silver medal for the fifth time in her career. But more importantly, she had gained an abundance of momentum heading into another Olympic year as the U.S. women prepared to compete in Beijing.

However, years of wear and tear had

taken their toll on her body. She has undergone seven surgeries during her athletic career, including operations on both shoulders and knees. "I had some injuries, and I was hurting in 2008. My shoulder was pretty torn up. I fought through a lot of injuries during my career and the timing obviously wasn't great for that to happen."

She finished fourth at the 2008 U.S. Open before falling to two-time World bronze medalist Katie Downing in the challenge tournament finals at the Olympic Trials in Las Vegas. "Yes, 2008 was rough. That's the only way to put it. It was rough."

She later went on to compete in college and study at Oklahoma City University, where she wrestled on the women's varsity team and won two national collegiate titles.

She made a record tenth U.S. World Team competing as Kristie Davis in 2010, but did not reach the podium after medaling in her nine previous appearances at Worlds. "Kristie is probably the best competitor I have ever been around, and that includes men and women," said Steiner. "There were so many times you thought she was out of a match and she found a way to win. She was just a winner and she found ways to win matches. I don't think it was because of great wrestling skill — she just knew how to win. That's Kristie in a nutshell."

Marano continued to compete, off and on, into her late 30s, wrestling at the 2012 and 2016 Olympic Trials, when she and Kayla attempted to become the first mother-daughter tandem to wrestle in the same Olympic Trials. Kayla, who won a Cadet World bronze medal in 2015, was unable to qualify for the event while her 37-year-old mother won her first match before going 2-2 in the tournament.

Kristie Davis, as she's now known, is employed as a registered nurse and lives in Georgia with her family. Her husband, Link Davis, is the head women's coach at Emmanuel College in Franklin Springs. Their daughter, Lilly, was born in 2009 and has started to compete in wrestling.

Those 10 World Championships appearances, nine World medals and seven trips to the World finals remain American records. She is one of only three U.S. women to win at least two World titles. "I have everything I want. I have a great family and I have a career that I love. Would it have been nice to make an Olympic team? Of course. But I know in my heart that I always did my best and I always competed my hardest. I really enjoyed wrestling and I still love the sport. Everything I did in wrestling made me the hard worker I am and gave me the drive I have to be successful in my life today."

The sport of women's wrestling has

come a long way since she won her first medal two decades ago, but still faces its share of obstacles. "Some things haven't changed. I went to a tournament that my daughter wrestled in and I heard several times, 'Oh, so-and-so has to wrestle a girl. What if he loses to her?' That really irked me, some 20 years after I started wrestling. Didn't we just go down this road 20 years ago? We should be well past that. I was fortunate that this never happened to me because of my backfround. But even as women's wrestling has grown, some of the stigma of a boy having to wrestle a girl, and possibly lose to her, is still there.

"It is great to see the opportunities that the girls have now. There are over 25 colleges out there that have a women's wrestling team. Girls now have more of the same scholarship opportunities that the guys do. They just have to wrestle the guys [in high school] to get it. Women's wrestling has grown tremendously. I would just like to see it grow a little more."

CHAPTER 6
Athens: The 2004 Olympics

Sara McMann was going to be the first. The trailblazer who would become the first American to capture an Olympic gold medal in women's freestyle wrestling. She was among the wide-eyed and eager participants who earned a shot at competing when women's wrestling made its debut on the Olympic Games program in 2004 in Athens, Greece.

The powerful McMann advanced to the semifinals and a matchup opposite hometown favorite Stavroula Zigouri of Greece. McMann came out on the attack, lifting and then planting Zigouri on her back with an explosive double-leg shot, scoring a stunning and decisive first-period fall just 50 seconds into the match.

In the process she made history by becoming the first American woman to land a spot in the Olympic finals.

Now she was just six minutes away from becoming Team USA's first female Olympic champion. Her opponent in the finals at 63 kilograms/138.75 pounds was the talented young star Kaori Icho of Japan.

McMann wasn't even favored to make the Olympic team. She was pinned by returning World champion Kristie Marano at 63 kilos in April's U.S. Open and was considered a slight underdog going into the Olympic Trials in Indianapolis. Marano had won a World title at 67 kilograms/147.5 pounds in 2003 while McMann had lost to Icho 4-3 in the finals at 63 kilograms.

When McMann arrived at weigh-ins, the day before competition, she heard the news that had quickly started circulating around the RCA Dome. Marano, who had cut down from a higher weight class to compete at 63 kilograms, was unable to make weight for the trials.

Sara McMann faces up to Japan's Icho at the 2007 World Championships. Larry Slater

With Marano forced to bump up a weight class, McMann rolled to the championship at the trials and punched her ticket to Athens.

Five-and-a-half years before she stepped on the mat to wrestle in the Olympic finals, an 18-year-old McMann experienced something nobody should ever have to endure. Her older brother, Jason, disappeared in January 1999 after reportedly being in an altercation with several football players at Lock Haven University in Pennsylvania.

Three months later, his body was found along a stream in a wooded area 30 miles away from where the altercation took place. McMann, just 21 years old, had been murdered. Sara's mentor and role model was gone.

After a police investigation stalled, the McMann family told their story on the television show *America's Most Wanted*. A tip called into the show, more than three years after the murder, led to the arrest of former Lock Haven football player Fabian Smart.

"You feel like something's been ripped away from you," McMann said in 2004. "I thought about revenge and stuff like that. A lot of my good wres-

Sara McMann endured the loss of her brother and fiancé during her wrestling career. WIN Magazine

tling came out of this, because I ducked my head and worked and worked and worked until I didn't think about it as much."

She eventually poured herself back into the sport in which she had started competing as a 14-year-old, joining an all-boys high school team at McDowell High School in Marion, North Carolina.

"My mom didn't want me to do it. She knew it was a tough sport and there weren't any other girls doing it."

McMann recalled a coach telling her mother, "It will be a cold day in hell before a girl wrestles in high school here."

That day arrived in 1994 when McMann walked into her first high school practice as a freshman. "When people started saying I shouldn't wrestle and got some resistance, that's when my mom got on board. I think we were determined to prove we could do it."

In her first week of practice, coach

Tim Hutchins was putting his team through what was actually called Hell Week, designed to help prepare his team for the tough physical rigors of the upcoming season.

And all eyes were on McMann to see if she would even survive the first week. "I had to prove I was a legitimate athlete and that I belonged there. The coach didn't think I should be there, so he made the hell week of conditioning the toughest ever. It was an unbelievably tough week. We went on long runs, did pushups, sit-ups and sprawls, ran sprints — a little bit of everything. It was intense, intense conditioning, and all of the freshmen were dying, but he didn't make me quit."

Hutchins wasn't crazy about a girl being on his team, but he gave McMann the same opportunity as everyone else. "The coach was very fair to me. I won him over because I did everything exactly the way he asked me to do it. He eventually became open-minded and accepted me onto the team. The fairness helped me thrive. I earned my spot on the team and earned that respect."

The first competitive match of McMann's career wasn't exactly fair, though. She was matched up against a three-year varsity starter in her first match. "It was horrible — he pinned me in 10 seconds. He was more experienced and stronger than me."

McMann had a second match that day, and won 10-3 at 125 pounds. "They put me up against a boy who was at my experience level. That was good for me. I learned early on to focus on smaller goals. I never got too discouraged from the losses. They made me sad and made me upset, but I was determined to improve.

"I really became passionate about wrestling. You would work on all these different techniques. The constant variety really appealed to me. The one-on-one and doing it on my own is something that appealed to me. I liked how hard it was. When I left those practices, I felt like I had accomplished something because of the unbelievable hard work I put in. I was really addicted to it."

McMann said she spent her first two years of high school wrestling "just trying to survive."

"It was difficult, and I wasn't the only one who went through that. There were other freshman and sophomores going through the same thing. What was fun was having the hard work pay off.

"There was never any thought of quitting. Once I made my mind up, that was it. I didn't love it the first year, but I made my mind up that there was no way I could quit. I am very stubborn, but I was very eager to learn. I was always raising my hand and asking questions. I always wanted to know the very smallest details and learn things thoroughly."

McMann continued to improve and

went 11-19 as a junior while competing only against boys. Her senior year she compiled a 15-13 record at 130 pounds "I was one match away from going to state. I lost a close match, and I was pretty sad. Looking back, I wouldn't trade that experience for anything. I really had to earn my place on the team and it was great to be accepted by the guys on the team."

McMann didn't plan on competing after high school, but she did receive a taste of Senior-level competition as a 16-year-old, competing for the first time against women at the 1996 U.S. Open in Orlando, Florida. One of her first opponents was an established Senior-level wrestler named Lauren Wolfe.

"Lauren just annihilated me. I shot in on a single leg, and I didn't realize what was going on. She had turned me to my back and kept exposing my back to the mat. I was new to freestyle wrestling and I didn't know to let go of the leg. She was fifth in the Worlds that year. It was a good lesson for me."

McMann came back to finish sixth at the U.S. Open. "It was an eye-opening experience. And it wasn't too horrible for a 16-year-old."

McMann earned a spot on her first U.S. Senior World team in 2000. In what would be a portent of things to come, she received a tough draw at her first World Championships, landing in a pool with five-time World champion Nikola Hartmann of Austria.

McMann opened with a 37-second pin over Greece's Sofia Kampanari before falling 5-2 to Hartmann. Only the winner advanced out of the pool, and Hartmann went on to a win a World title at 62 kilograms/136.5 pounds.

Another bad draw came at the 2001 Worlds when McMann landed in the same pool with two-time World champion Lili Meng of China, who won the tournament. "She beat me pretty bad, so I didn't get out of my pool."

In 2002, McMann was in a three-person pool with a top young wrestler from Japan who would become one of the greatest of all time. McMann opened with an 11-0 technical fall over Yoon So-Young of Korea before facing Japan's Kaori Icho.

Icho defeated McMann en route to winning her first of 10 World titles. It would be the first big matchup of many between the two stars. "I had some really bad luck with my draws. What would be the odds of me having the World champion in my pool three years in a row? But those tough draws helped me when I got to the Olympics."

When her pool came out for the 2004 Olympics, McMann's first match was against Meng, who had beaten her three years before.

There were three wrestlers in her pool with the winner advancing to the semifinal round of the Olympics. Canada's Viola Yanik was the third member of the pool at 63 kilograms/138.75 pounds.

Tricia Saunders, one of the U.S. Olympic coaches in 2004, had helped prepare McMann for a situation like this. "Tricia had me visualize what the worst-case scenario would be for me and come to terms with it. So when I drew China for my first match, I was ready. She beat me badly in 2001, but I was a different wrestler in 2004. I had improved a lot since then."

McMann flipped the script and became the bad draw for Meng, building an early 2-0 lead before taking Meng to her back and recording a fall late in the first period.

McMann jumped to her feet and pumped her fist in celebration. "I normally didn't celebrate like that, but I knew how big of a win that was for me. I had the biggest rush of adrenaline I had ever had in my life. I was so happy."

McMann had a bye in the second round and watched as Meng came back strong, rolling to a lopsided 8-0 win over Yanik. McMann was in the driver's seat now heading into the third and final round of the pool matches against the Canadian.

"I had beaten Yanik 10 times — I had never lost to her. Going into the match, I knew all I had to do was not get pinned and I would win my pool. For some reason, I didn't have it in me for that match against Canada. I was almost wrestling not to get pinned. I wanted to win, but I couldn't mentally get myself to do it."

Down 5-0 to Yanik after the first period, McMann came back to score two takedowns before dropping the match 5-2. "I didn't even care about the loss to Canada. I know it sounds weird, but it didn't bother me. All that mattered was that I won my pool and I was in the semifinals of the Olympics. I still had a chance to accomplish my goals."

McMann followed with the quick semifinal fall over Zigouri. "I had wrestled her before and she was very, very strong, and I was more scared by her than any other girl because of that. I had everything to lose. She had qualified for the Olympics because her country was hosting the Games. Otherwise she wouldn't have even qualified."

Backed by a boisterous crowd, Zigouri shot in first on a double leg and lifted McMann off the mat. But McMann fought her off before striking with a double-leg shot of her own that resulted in a pin in the match's first minute. She showed little emotion after the win, which had clinched her an Olympic medal.

"She had lifted me and that pissed me off. That really got me going. I came right back, and hit an arm drag and doubled her and pinned her."

McMann had reached the pinnacle of her career when she stepped onto the

Sara McMann suffered a tough loss to the great Kaori Icho in the 2004 Olympics.

mat to face Icho in the Olympic gold-medal match. "I wanted a gold medal. I had clinched a silver, but I wasn't even thinking about that. I wasn't satisfied at all about being in the finals. I had trained 10 years to be an Olympic champion. I had wrestled Icho at the 2003 World finals and lost in overtime. I knew I was really close to realizing my dream of winning the Olympics. That year between the Worlds and the Olympics, I tried to improve in every area I could — technique, training, nutrition. We watched video of my matches with Icho and looked for any edge that we could find. I put everything I had into my preparations to beat her."

McMann charged out aggressively, as was customary, and collected a passivity warning for stalling against Icho midway through the first period. She followed with a pair of one-point takedowns, including a single-leg attack with seven seconds left in the period. That gave McMann a 2-0 lead heading into the 30-second break.

She was right on track to capture an Olympic gold medal.

The second three-minute period began and McMann's lead was cut in half on an Icho takedown a minute into the period. Icho tied it 2-2 after a quick single-leg attack resulted in a takedown with one minute remaining in the match. The bout was still tied 2-2 with under 30 seconds to go. Icho barreled in on a double-leg shot and scooted behind McMann for a takedown with 0:24 left. McMann tried valiantly to score in the final seconds, but time ran out.

Icho jumped up and down before running over to celebrate with her coaches, while McMann stood with her head down and her hands on her hips. She fought back tears on the medal podium as the Japanese national anthem played and the flags of the medalists from each country were raised. It was a crushing defeat.

"Sara wrestled really well in 2003, and then she took it up another level in 2004," coach Terry Steiner said. "She was ready to win the Olympics. She got off to a great start in the finals against

Icho. Looking back, there were some questionable calls where we should've had more points. But take nothing away from Icho. She's a great champion, and she's shown that time and again. Sara was definitely on top of her game at that time. She should've won that match."

Icho went on to become one of the most decorated wrestlers in history in any style, adding Olympic gold medals in 2008, 2012 and 2016.

Just two weeks after the Athens Olympics, Sara McMann endured another tragedy. She had just traveled home from Athens to Colorado Springs, where she had been a resident-athlete at the U.S. Olympic Training Center.

McMann and her fiancé, Steve Blackford, an All-American wrestler for Arizona State, were planning to move to Washington, D.C. He was enrolled in law school there and she was planning to pursue a master's degree. They embarked on their journey late in the morning on September 3, 2004. They planned to stop in Blackford's hometown of Des Moines, Iowa, and spend Labor Day at a family barbecue in the capital city of Iowa.

A few hours into the drive, the Jeep Cherokee that McMann was driving and Blackford was riding in went off the road on Interstate 76 near Brush, Colorado. The truck rolled onto its side and then tumbled down an embankment, rolling over twice. Neither McMann nor

Patricia Miranda wrestled in the 2004 Olympics

Blackman were wearing seat belts, and both were ejected from the vehicle.

McMann suffered a broken arm, but otherwise wasn't seriously injured. Blackford's body, however, had crashed through the passenger side window. He reportedly landed about 30 feet from the truck. By the time help arrived at the scene, Blackford had died. He was just 27 years old.

Still heartbroken, McMann eventually found her way back to the wrestling mat. She made three more U.S. World Teams, earning World bronze medals in 2005 and 2007.

McMann was favored to make her second straight Olympic team in 2008, but Randi Miller defeated McMann for the spot on the American squad.

McMann eventually embarked on a career in mixed martial arts. She won the first seven fights of her MMA career

...before going to Yale Law School. *WIN Magazine*

to earn a shot at world champion Ronda Rousey at UFC 170 in 2014 in Las Vegas. McMann lost by first-round TKO before bouncing back to win her next fight in the Ultimate Fighting Championships

McMann fell to Miesha Tate, another fighter with a wrestling pedigree, by majority decision in early 2015 in Las Vegas. Tate went on to become a UFC world champion in 2016.

In those same 2004 Olympics, Patricia Miranda clinched a bronze, becoming the first American woman to win an Olympic medal. She fell to three-time World champion Irini Merleni of Ukraine by a 9-0 score in the semifinals. Merleni earned the honor of becoming the first Olympic gold medalist in women's wrestling.

In the bronze-medal bout at 48 kilograms/105.5 pounds, Miranda rallied from an early 4-0 deficit to down France's Angelique Berthenet 12-4. Miranda was thrown with a headlock early in the bout, but she stormed back with a combination of takedowns and gut-wrenches to win pulling away.

"Winning a medal definitely helps, in that it's an honor to see your flag raised, to see your country represented, to look genuinely happy to have been able to have clashed heads with the best in the world," Miranda said after the 2004 medal ceremony. "I do have to say that the six-hour period between the semifinals and my third and fourth match was probably one of the hardest I've had in my sport. Every time I go to bed I see gold. But, there is some pride."

Miranda started wrestling growing up in California, and became a varsity starter on the men's team at Stanford. She made an immediate impact internationally, placing second at the 2000 and 2003 World Championships.

An outstanding student, Miranda was accepted to Yale Law School, but she deferred her admission to Yale to train for the 2004 Olympics. After making them, Miranda gained significant media attention since women's wrestling was competing for the first time in an Olympic Games. The team was profiled in publications such as *ESPN* magazine, *Time* and *People* while bringing awareness to the sport.

She took 2005 off to study at Yale Law School and returned to competition in 2006, winning a World bronze medal. She was favored to make a second straight Olympic team in 2008, but lost to Clarissa Chun in the final round of the Olympic Trials.

Miranda has gone on to a successful career as a lawyer. "Patricia's the gold standard," Steiner said. "She's one of these people who is very intelligent and very driven. She's the type of person who is going to excel at whatever she does."

Miranda gained her position on the U.S. squad after winning the historic first Olympic Trials held in May, 2004. She swept two straight matches in the best-of-three finals over the promising Chun.

The U.S. finished with two medals in the four weight classes contested in Athens. It remains the best performance by the U.S. women in four Olympic Games appearances.

Americans Tela O'Donnell and Toccara Montgomery also were part of that four-member Olympic squad.

O'Donnell placed sixth in Athens after knocking off two-time World silver medalist Tina George to make the Olympic team. George had won her medals in the two previous years, in 2002 and 2003, but lost by fall to O'Donnell in both bouts of the Olympic Trials finals.

Montgomery won World silver medals in 2001 and 2003 before placing seventh in the 2004 Olympics. To make the U.S. Olympic team, Montgomery had downed Kristie Marano at the trials in two close matches.

"It was exciting obviously, having women's wrestling in the Olympics for the first time. It was very special," Steiner said. "The first Olympics was really challenging. People put so much into it and there was so much buildup for that event. We had good success at the Olympics. But we had four finalists at the four Olympic weights at the 2003 World Championships, so it was also bittersweet because we had really high expectations in 2004."

Montgomery, from Cleveland, Ohio, was a wrestler who excelled at a very young age and overcame her own share of adversity to excel. When she was 15 years old, her father Paul was convicted of a double murder.

Paul Montgomery was going to visit his brother on October 3, 1998 when two men confronted him on the sidewalk and offered to sell him drugs. Paul passed on the offer and an argument ensued. One of the men pulled out a gun — Paul says he wrestled the gun away in the struggle that followed, then shot the two men and ran off in a panic.

Paul drove home and told his wife, Tara, what had happened. Toccara and her younger brother Patrick, six, were in bed asleep. Later that night, Paul saw policemen searching the neighborhood

The powerful Toccara Montgomery had a brief, but successful, wrestling career. USA Wrestling

and turned himself in.

The gunshot victims died and Paul was charged with two counts of murder — he was found guilty and jailed for 30 years to life.

Montgomery kept her emotions bottled up following the shootings, immersing herself in school and with her friends. When her father first went away, she was upset and refused to speak with him when he would call from prison. But they would rebuild their relationship over time.

Later that year, she heard an announcement at school that the new wrestling coach, Kip Flanik, was looking for athletes to join the squad. Thirty boys signed up for team and so did five girls, including Montgomery, an honor roll student who was gifted athletically and very eager to learn about her new sport.

Flanik realized right away he had someone special to work with. "When Kip pushed me, I said 'This man is not going to make me quit,'" Montgomery said. "Once I realized he was trying to make me better, I not only respected him, but I liked him better."

The powerful and explosive Montgomery caught on quickly and she was soon making an impact on the national and international levels. She was just 18 when she won a silver medal at the 2001 Junior World Championships. A couple of months later, she advanced to the finals of the 2001 Senior World Championships at 68 kilograms/149.5 pounds, facing five-time World champion Christine Nordhagen of Canada, a member of the United World Wrestling Hall of Fame.

Nordhagen defeated Montgomery, but the teenager turned in an eye-opening performance. Two years later, Montgomery again advanced to the World finals, at 158.5 pounds, and again lost to an experienced opponent, Kyoko Hamaguchi of Japan.

Prior to the 2004 Olympics, Montgomery was asked about her father, who she visited twice a year in prison. "I don't really want to go into that. It has nothing to do with my wrestling."

But she did open up in another interview later that year. "I have a better relationship with my dad than some people do who see their dad every day under their roof. He is hoping to be able to see me on TV during the Olympics. I am hoping so."

Coach Steiner said the experience helped Montgomery find perspective. "Probably nothing seems as big as what she's had to handle in her personal life. It's just a wrestling match — it's not going to define who she is."

With wrestlers not seeded in international events, Montgomery drew Hamaguchi again in her first match at the 2004 Olympics, losing 4-1. Montgomery came back to pin Bulgaria's

Stanka Zlateva in her next match, but did not advance out of her pool — Zlateva went on to capture five World titles.

Montgomery was just 21 when she stepped away from competition, but she remained involved — in 2010 she became head women's coach at Lindenwood University in Saint Charles, Missouri.

McMann continues to compete, while raising her young daughter, Bella, and is still ranked among the top 10 fighters in the world. She improved her MMA career record to 9-3 after earning a unanimous decision over Jessica Eye in a UFC bout in May, 2016 in Las Vegas.

In 2004, one of the women's team coaches was Tricia Saunders, who recently made some observations about that experience. "I got into coaching, but it was tough on me because I also was working full-time. I would get four weeks of vacation a year, but I had to use all four weeks to prepare the team for the Athens Olympics. It was hard to be gone for the entire month. I had a family to raise as well.

"That was a good month though. There were some talented athletes. There was a lot of pressure being the first women's team in the Olympics. We didn't have anyone on the team who was winning tournaments really consistently like some of the Japanese women.

"I liked those girls on the U.S. team in 2004 so much and I wanted them to win so badly. When they don't win, you suffer and you know how bad it feels. You have trained for years and sometimes it's just a small mistake here and there that causes you to lose your dream."

During that Olympics debut year, USA Wrestling picked up an important sponsor which has played a key role in the sport. Arno Niemand, who wrestled for Cornell University in the 1950s, founded a company in Boulder, Colorado in 1990. It is called Body Bar Systems and provides products and educational tools for fitness enthusiasts.

Prior to the 2004 Olympics, Niemand was approached about Body Bar being a sponsor for the sport's national governing body. Body Bar became an important new sponsor for USA Wrestling. Niemand asked USA Wrestling marketing guru Larry Nugent if there were any specific areas where they were looking for help.

"The women's team," Nugent responded.

"I was kind of taken aback at first because I had never focused on the women's side at all," Niemand said. "However, I recognized that it dovetailed nicely with Body Bar, which was principally featuring products that were used by women in the aerobic studios for strength training. It seemed to me to be a perfect fit."

The Body Bar partnership has been a successful one. USA Wrestling has hosted a Body Bar event, a female national tournament for age-group girls, for more than a decade. Among the young girls who have won Body Bar titles are three-time World champion Adeline Gray and Olympic and World champion Helen Maroulis.

Sara McMann was selected in 2004 to be the first spokesperson for Body Bar. "That worked out very well for Body Bar," Niemand said. "Seeing Sara win an Olympic medal was gratifying."

Just prior to the 2004 Games, the women's wrestling team was invited to ring the opening bell at the New York Stock Exchange one morning. Saunders was there along with Patricia Miranda. Niemand's colleague, Sherry Catlin from Body Bar, also was there.

"It was good fortune that John Thain, former president of Goldman Sachs, was head of the New York Stock Exchange at that time," Niemand said. "That was a day we will always remember."

Marcie Van Dusen, a 2008 Olympian, succeeded McMann as spokesperson for Body Bar.

"Marcie did a really nice job for us," Niemand said. He also fondly remembered working with two-time World medalist Sally Roberts and Olympian Tela O'Donnell. "Sally was a free spirit who was really great, and Tela was absolutely terrific."

Niemand, who is now retired, has fond memories of his association with Body Bar and the American women's wrestling team. "It was very gratifying to see the success and the growth of the U.S. women's program. It has come a long way. But it still has a long way to go to reach the potential for wrestling to be a sport for both genders."

CHAPTER 7
Coach Terry Steiner

Terry Steiner was looking for a way out. As his sixth season as an assistant coach at the University of Wisconsin came to a close, the 32-year-old Steiner turned to his wife, Jodi, during the 2002 NCAA Wrestling Championships in Albany, New York. "I need to make a change," he said.

His professional dream was to become a head coach at the NCAA Division I level. When the job at Cal State Fullerton came open, Steiner placed a call to USA Wrestling Executive Director Rich Bender.

"I'm applying for this position," Steiner told Bender. "Would you write a letter of recommendation for me?"

Bender's response caught Steiner by surprise.

"Sure, I can do that," Bender replied. "But what about the women's coaching position?"

Steiner had no idea what Bender was talking about, but in the spring of 2002 USA Wrestling was looking to hire its first full-time national coach for women's wrestling.

In the fall of 2001, the International Olympic Committee had announced it was adding women's wrestling to the Olympic Games program beginning in 2004. USA Wrestling, the sport's national governing body, also was starting a resident program for the women at the U.S. Olympic Training Center in Colorado Springs, Colorado.

"I didn't know anything about it and didn't know much about women's wrestling," Steiner said. "I never paid attention to it. I was really reluctant."

Bender continued with his pitch to Steiner. "Will you listen to us?" Bender said.

"I'll listen," Steiner said. When he returned to his Madison, Wisconsin

Terry Steiner has been the head coach of the USA Wrestling National Women's team since 2002. John Sachs

Terry Steiner wrestling at Iowa, where he was an NCAA champion. *University of Iowa*

home that night, he informed his wife about the women's coaching job at USA Wrestling.

"Why wouldn't you look at it?" Jodi Steiner said.

"Did you hear what I just said?" Steiner fired back.

"Yes, I heard you," she said. "But why wouldn't you look at it? It's a great opportunity in the sport of wrestling."

Steiner walked out of the house, shaking his head. "I thought to myself, 'Well, she doesn't understand,'" he said.

Seeking a second opinion, he drove a mile down the road to his twin brother Troy's place. "Title IX was such a big issue at that time. I was worried if I took that job in women's wrestling, I would never be able to get back to college wrestling."

His twin brother offered a different perspective. "If you come back into college wrestling, you're not going to be hired by college coaches, you're going to be hired by college administrators because they will know you can work with everyone," Troy told his brother that night.

"I remember walking out of Troy's place and thinking, 'Damn, the two people I relied on the most, they're not helping.' I was looking for a way out and they weren't giving it to me. I was 32 years old and no longer competing at that point. I had to ask myself, 'Why do I want to stay in wrestling? Is it for the money, is it for fame and fortune?'

"I believe in wrestling. It's a sport I know and love. Because of some of the things I accomplished maybe people will listen to me. I believe in the sport of wrestling and what it can teach — character development and human development. My next question was: what difference does it make if I'm coaching a man or a woman?"

A later conversation with his wife provided even more perspective for Steiner. "What if your daughter wanted to wrestle, and follow in your footsteps?"

"That was the point in the conversation," Steiner said, "where I thought this was the right thing to do."

Three weeks after Bender first mentioned the job to Steiner, he was hired as USA Wrestling's first full-time national coach for women's freestyle wrestling. "When I first walked in the wrestling room, I didn't know any of the girls. I had to introduce myself and try to get to know them."

His own path in the sport began in his hometown of Bismarck, the North Dakota state capital and a city of 67,000 people located in the central part of the state. Terry and Troy entered the world on August 27, 1969. At their first official weigh-in, the identical Steiner twins weighed 2.2 and 2.4 pounds. "Troy was born first, seven minutes ahead of me — I kicked him out," Steiner said.

Their parents, Tim and Lil, were both just 18 years old at the time. "We were born right after they finished high school. My parents didn't get married until a year and four months later because they wanted to make sure it was right for them. We started out living with my mom at my grandma's house. My dad lived with his parents.

"People were saying it wouldn't work and didn't give them a chance. But they made it work. They found ways to do it and make the best of the situation. They went right to work to support their family. My mom and dad didn't have perfect lives. They were hard-working people who tried to do their best and were pretty successful at everything they did. We didn't have to look far to see hard workers who helped people. That was my parents — they modeled the way for us."

His father worked as a mechanic and his mother owned a salon. "We lived at the salon half the time. It was a family business and we were always there. My dad was there a lot when he wasn't working. My brother and my sister, Trasi, were there.

"I always say if I wasn't a wrestling coach, I would be a hairstylist. I know I would have been. Our family was in the hair business and that's what I would've done."

Steiner said early in his career his father, who wrestled in high school, came down on him after he lost a match in fifth grade. Steiner had lost to Terry Brands, who later was a teammate of Steiner's at Iowa. Brands went on to win two World titles and an Olympic bronze medal. "I was upset after the match and my dad yelled at me. He came back a short time later and apologized to me. He was smart enough to realize what it did to me. He was upset because I got beat, but he never did that again. Never. He was supportive. He said to me, 'If you're going to do something, do the best you can.' My mom and dad were just encouraging and supportive, and that was exactly what Troy and I needed."

A turning point for the Steiner twins came in high school. Randy Lewis, a two-time NCAA champion for Iowa and a 1984 Olympic gold medalist, came to North Dakota to work a wrestling camp. Lewis met the Steiners and then invited them to his camp in his hometown of Rapid City, South Dakota.

"It happened to be at the same time that Randy's sister was getting married to [former Iowa wrestler] Jeff Kerber, so all of the Iowa wrestlers were there. We became very familiar with Iowa wrestling during that time."

Among the Hawkeye wrestlers the Steiners met were three-time NCAA champion Jim Zalesky, NCAA champion Brad Penrith and All-American Greg Randall. The Steiners attended a two-week camp at the University of Iowa after their junior year in high school.

After Lewis watched the Steiners wrestle, he returned with a message to legendary Iowa coach Dan Gable. "You need to get these guys," Lewis told Gable. "If you don't, it might haunt you a little bit."

Lewis continued to push Gable to sign the Steiner twins. "If you think that much of them," Gable said, "let's go look at them."

The Steiners had attended J Robinson's grueling 28-day intensive camp after their freshman year of high school and had narrowed their choices to Iowa and Minnesota.

"J's the type of guy you get to know very quickly," Steiner said. "He was very communicative." Robinson was in his early years as Minnesota's head coach after being a long-time assistant to Gable when Iowa became a national powerhouse.

The first Division I college match Steiner saw in person came his senior year in high school when he attended the Iowa-Minnesota dual meet in Minneapolis.

During their senior year, the Steiners traveled to Iowa on a recruiting visit. "Wrestling was very important at Iowa. You were kind of in awe of everything. They were the premier program in the country."

On the trip home from Iowa to North Dakota, the Steiners had to fly through Minneapolis. "When we arrived at the gate at the airport in Minneapolis, J Robinson was there. It was really hard trying to decide between Iowa and Minnesota. We were really split. Troy was leaning one way and I was leaning the other way. We wanted to stay together. Minnesota offered us a full ride and Iowa offered us tuition. We were elated when Iowa offered us tuition."

The Steiners ultimately chose Iowa, and placed a tough call to Robinson. "We were in more than a recruiting battle — we were in a war between J Robinson and Dan Gable. J was upset and understandably so. He put a lot of time and energy into recruiting us. It was hard. We never chose Gable over Robinson. We chose Iowa over Minnesota. Iowa was more established at that point, and we wanted to give ourselves the best shot. I would like to think we could've gone to Minnesota and accomplished the same things we did at Iowa. J had only been at Minnesota for just a few years, but you could see that he was building something special."

The Steiner twins came to Iowa at a time when Gable's recruiting philosophy was undergoing some changes. Iowa had won nine straight NCAA team titles from 1978-86, but the favored Hawkeyes finished second in 1987 and 1988. This would've been more than good enough for most programs, but not the Gable-led Iowa teams.

Hawkeye teams were known for working hard on the mat, but also had become known for playing just as hard off the mat. "Gable had to make some changes," Steiner said. "He always had talented and hard-working guys, but there were off-the-mat issues with a lot of guys getting in trouble and partying too much. Before then, Gable was recruiting 'talent.' They were doing some things all wrong, but they were still winning so he couldn't say a lot because they were winning with their talent.

"Gable changed his recruiting approach and changed the culture of the program with the type of kids he was recruiting. That started when Tom and Terry Brands came in the year before we did."

The Brands brothers combined to win five NCAA titles, three World titles and an Olympic title. Tom Brands is now the head coach and Terry the associate head coach at Iowa. Iowa has won three NCAA team titles under Tom Brands.

"Gable realized he had to recruit more than just on talent," Steiner said. "He understood he also had to start recruiting on attitude and work ethic and discipline and structure. And that's what he got with the Brands and my brother and me. During our time there, I think there was a huge respect for what people were doing on a daily basis. It was a very close-knit team from that standpoint."

The changes weren't immediately evident. The Hawkeyes were sixth at the 1989 NCAAs and third in 1990, as Oklahoma State won back-to-back national titles. But Iowa's fortunes were about to turn around — and in a big way by winning the NCAA team championships in 1991, 1992 and 1993.

As with many incoming freshmen, the Steiners struggled in their first days in the loaded Iowa wrestling room — Troy Steiner competed at 142 pounds, Terry at 150. "I don't know if I scored a point in my first three months in the Iowa wrestling room," Steiner said. "There were so many great wrestlers in there — not just the college guys, but the international guys who were training for the Worlds and the Olympics. Steve Martin, who was a 118-pounder, was even kicking my butt. And then probably everyone else up through John Heffernan at 167.

"Those guys would kick your ass, but at the end of the day they would help you and pick you back up and take you back through it. You realize it's a process. There was an expectation and a standard there. We didn't question anything. They could've told me to do 100 matches a day and I would've gone and done it. I did everything they told me. I went through a big transformation there, to really struggling early and then after being there two years thinking I can't be beat by anybody. That's a credit to what Gable built and the atmosphere he created there."

Steiner said Gable was "a man of few words. But when he said something, everyone listened. I remember one time Greg Randall was back for a college football weekend, and I asked him if he wanted to work out. Gable sat there the whole practice and watched. Greg got the better of me, for sure. I'm walking into the locker room and when I was passing Gable he said, 'You're going to have to get a lot tougher than that if you want to get where you want to get.' I remember I went home, and I couldn't sleep and I couldn't eat. I was so upset by that. That's all he said. I was redshirting, and it was my first year there.

"The next day, I wrestled Greg again. I did better and I held my own a little bit more. Gable was there again watching and he never said a word during the workout. When I was walking to the locker room after practice he said, 'Difference of night and day.' Gable didn't have to say a lot. You didn't get a pat on the back all the time or get told how great you were doing. That worked for me. He found ways like that to motivate people. If you did get a pat on the back, it felt so good. You yearned for that.

"We had a room full of people who were really good. If you didn't do the job, you knew there was somebody right behind you who could do it for you. It wasn't a wrestling room for everyone. If you needed a lot of personal attention and constant pats on the back and praise, that wasn't the room. They kind of threw you out there in the wrestling room and it was the survival of the fittest."

Steiner learned another early lesson during his redshirt year when Iowa returned home after losing to Michigan in the finals of a conference, multi-team dual-meet. "During the course of the event, Iowa got called for stalling quite a few times in the three dual meets. That next week, we had a tough two-hour practice with a lot of live wrestling. After practice, Gable said, 'Okay, put your running shoes on.' We went up to the top of Carver-Hawkeye Arena and we had to run one sprint lap for every stalling call they got.

"Gable pointed out each stalling call for each lap we ran. 'This lap is for the stalling call in this match.' I remember one of my teammates saying to me, 'Wait until he gets to the Michigan dual.' When we started doing laps, I didn't know exactly how many times they had been called for stalling. But I quickly learned they had been called six times for stalling against Michigan because we ran six sprint laps. I just remember we kept running and running. We ended up running a total of 12 sprint laps for a total of 12 stalling calls. That was a very rough day. It was tough, but we did the workout. We trusted Gable. If he would've asked us to run 24 laps, we would've done 24."

As you might have imagined, Iowa wasn't called for stalling in its next dual meet. "Obviously, the team hadn't been wrestling aggressively like Gable's teams typically did. Gable was upset and wanted to send a message to the team. I think the message was pretty clearly received."

Steiner eventually broke into the powerful Iowa lineup, placing third at the 1991 NCAAs and fifth in 1992, while Troy won an NCAA title at 142 pounds in 1992.

Steiner entered the 1993 NCAA tournament in Ames, Iowa, as the second seed at 150 pounds behind top seed Troy Sunderland of Penn State. He stopped by Gable's office before the tournament. "This is how I see it," Gable told Steiner. "There are four people in your weight class that can win it. If you are going to separate yourself from them, you're going to have to take risks. You're going to have to open up and get after it. If you don't, then it's the flip of a coin."

It was typical Gable, not mincing words. "It was very matter-of-fact," Steiner said. "I had one week left in my college career and didn't have what I wanted. I knew it wasn't a time to hold back. It was a time to showcase what I could do."

Steiner did exactly that. He reached the finals before edging Sunderland 8-7 to cap his Hawkeye career with an NCAA title. He was named Outstanding Wrestler of the tournament. "Gable didn't have to say anything after I won — I knew how he felt. I was relieved I could finally do that for the university and for Coach Gable. They put a lot of time and resources and money into developing us. To finally accomplish that, it was a sense of relief for everyone. It was never all about winning. But Gable knew you weren't going to be happy without an NCAA title. He really cared about you as a person. That resonated with me. Every coach in there cared about us.

"That attitude was very evident when we got there. He got those kind of people in that wrestling room and things came together. During my years there, there were a lot of great people in that room. I think we respected everyone. We might not have always been buddy-buddy and hung out all the time with each other but there was a huge respect for what people were doing on a daily basis. It was a very close-knit team from that standpoint."

The Steiners had outstanding collegiate careers. Troy was a four-time All-American and 1992 NCAA champion for Iowa. Terry was a three-time All-

American and 1993 NCAA champion. They were members of three national championship teams and four Big Ten championship teams.

Steiner stayed at Iowa for one year after finishing his collegiate career. He then spent the next two seasons as an assistant coach at Oregon State. "I had a great experience at Oregon State. Joe Wells was the head coach, and he was a great mentor for me."

When Steiner arrived in Corvallis, Oregon, Wells had a question for him. "How do you want to help the program here?" Wells said.

"I know how to train and I know how to work," Steiner replied. "I can bring a work ethic and attitude and intensity to the room."

Wells then put Steiner in charge of the team's training. "It was a great opportunity for me, especially being only one year out of college. And then Joe taught me all of the other things — the administrative side, dealing with fundraising, booster club, recruiting, parents, how to run a program.

"You had to be a jack of all trades at a school like Oregon State. Joe taught me everything. I had a great experience. Randy Couture was there at that time — he brought a different philosophy coming from Oklahoma State, plus he had a strong Greco-Roman background. And then Les Gutches was on the team. He was a superstar in his own right, but he didn't know it yet. He didn't even know how good he was at that point."

Couture went on to become a UFC world champion in mixed martial arts while Gutches won two NCAA titles and a World freestyle title in wrestling.

Steiner then spent the next six seasons at Wisconsin before going to USA Wrestling in 2002.

The Steiner twins continued to compete internationally through 2000 — Terry placed fourth at the 1996 and 2000 Olympic Trials, while Troy twice placed third at the trials.

"I definitely never accomplished my goals at the Senior level," Steiner said. "I was pretty broken up about it." He was approached by Canada's Daniel Igali and American Lincoln McIlravy about being a training partner for them for the 2000 Olympic Games in Sydney, Australia. Steiner elected to help McIlravy, who was his college teammate at Iowa. Igali went on to win the Olympics and McIlravy placed third.

"What I learned at Iowa was if you can't win, do the next best thing," Steiner said. "Come back and get third or help someone else win. I made a decision to not be bitter moving forward. I decided that maybe helping someone else could heal some of my own wounds. So I decided to go help Lincoln. It was a good experience. That helped me realize life was going to go on. It was my first time at the Olympics. It was a great experience. Lincoln lost a really close match to Igali in the semifinals."

Steiner gave McIlravy a pep talk after that match. "You're going to leave here a lot happier with a medal than without one," Steiner told McIlravy. "Let's come back and get this."

Steiner remembered being with McIlravy shortly after he came back to win a bronze medal at the 2000 Olympics. "I was walking with Lincoln afterwards, and then seeing his kids. They were real young and they were sliding down a banister, and giggling and laughing and having fun. Then Lincoln looks at me and says, 'I guess it didn't affect them very much.' That was a great thing to see because that's life. Life goes on. Daniel Igali and Lincoln McIlravy were both great champions. Igali is probably the most athletic person I've ever wrestled."

A loss to Steiner actually provided a turning point in Igali's career. "Dave McKay, Igali's coach, credits that match for Igali's improvement. I got thrown on my back early in the match, but I ended up coming back to beat Igali in overtime. Igali said he had never been that tired in his life. After that, Dave worked a lot more with Igali on his conditioning."

Steiner had plenty of work to do when he assumed the leadership of the women's wrestling program in 2002. Shortly after he was hired, Steiner saw the U.S. win two medals at his first World Championships — Tina George with a silver medal and Kristie Marano a bronze.

With the 2003 World Championships set for New York City, Steiner knew his team had plenty of work to do. That event also would serve as a qualifier for the 2004 Olympics. "When I took the job, I said I would give it two years. I really thought after two years I would go back into college wrestling. After I took the job, I thought what can we change in two years? At that time, we had forced par terre. So we worked on that because we knew we could score a lot of points. Every one of our girls were good at turning people. We knew if we had good defense we could stay in matches and have chances to win. We made some big gains by working on those areas.

"For the girls, this was the first time they had a full-time coach and this level of commitment to women's wrestling with the Olympic Games coming up. It was a magical time."

The U.S. responded with a superb performance at the 2003 World Championships. Five wrestlers advanced to the finals and all seven American women won medals. Marano won a World title while George, Miranda, McMann and Montgomery each won silvers. Jenny Wong and Sally Roberts won bronze medals.

The U.S. tied Japan atop the team standings, though Japan won the team title by virtue of having more individual champions. "It was a great performance that caught a lot of people's attention and moved women's wrestling ahead a lot in one weekend," Steiner said. "It was affirmation for me that what we were doing was working, but we had some great athletes who wrestled really well."

The U.S. followed by winning two medals in the 2004 Olympics, with McMann earning a silver and Miranda a bronze.

Two years later, the close-knit Steiner family suffered a huge loss when Tim Steiner died at the age of 55 after a five-year battle with cancer. "It was a bad deal obviously," said Steiner. "He was way too young. It was very difficult when he passed. He was a pillar to our lives. He meant everything to us. He was such a generous and supportive father."

Steiner said he is constantly evolving as a coach. "There are differences in coaching men and coaching women. Sometimes it's the tone of how you say something and not necessarily the message. Every athlete is different. I've learned how to communicate better and get my message across more effectively. I've definitely made a lot of mistakes along the way, but I've also learned how to deal with situations better. I feel like I have a real purpose here with what I'm doing with women's wrestling."

Adeline Gray has worked closely with Steiner since she made her first World team in 2009. They haven't always seen eye-to-eye, but both coach and athlete have found an effective way to develop a productive relationship.

"Terry's very understanding and has a real knack for working with females," Gray said. "He's able to work outside his comfort zone sometimes of what's traditional. It's still a male-dominated sport, and I think for coaches to come over and coach women, it takes some adjusting. He's the best at it."

Brother Troy became a head coach at the NCAA Division I level in 2016 after taking over the reinstated wrestling program at Fresno State. "I am so happy for Troy," said Steiner. "It's a tremendous opportunity for him. It's a win-win for him and for Fresno State. I know he will do a great job. I was joking with him right after he got hired that the honeymoon was over and he better get to work."

The Steiner twins are fully aware of how impactful the sport of wrestling can be on a young person's life.

"Wrestling teaches you life skills — how to be disciplined, how to work hard to achieve a goal, how to deal with adversity, how to deal with stress, and how to handle life as it comes to you," Terry said. "Life's not easy. Wrestling teaches you so much. It is much more than winning and losing. Athletes have to walk away from a career with more than medals around their necks. They have to leave with an understanding of what the sport taught them about thriving in tough situations. Wrestling brings that strength and character out in you because it's a sport that tests you all the time. You are going to have to find a way to fight through tough situations. Wrestling prepares you very well for life."

CHAPTER 8
Beijing: The 2008 Olympics

Randi Miller had never made a World team and was relatively unknown on the international level. But she wasn't about to back down from anyone. Not after she beat an Olympic and World silver medalist to make the 2008 U.S. Olympic team in women's freestyle wrestling.

The 24-year-old Miller wasn't considered a serious medal contender when she walked onto the mat to compete at the 2008 Olympic Games in Beijing, China. But the powerful, hard-nosed Miller sent a resounding message in her first two matches that she was ready to battle. She scored a quick 40-second pin over Egypt's Haiat Farac in her first match and followed by earning a hard-fought, three-period win over Ukraine's Yuliya Ostapchuk in her second match.

Next up was a quarterfinal match with Kaori Icho of Japan. Miller dropped the first period 3-0 before losing by fall in the second period to Icho, who would go on to win her second of four Olympic gold medals. "It was embarrassing. There shouldn't be anybody in my weight class who can dominate me like that, but she was just better than me on that day. It wasn't a lack of effort on my part or a case of not being prepared. She was just better."

Miller battled back to pin Azerbaijan's Olesya Zamula to land a spot in the bronze medal match and a showdown against veteran Martine Dugrenier of Canada, a three-time World silver medalist. It was the biggest match of her life.

Miller, who grew up in Arlington, Texas, followed an interesting path to the Olympics after starting wrestling as a 16-year-old. Just 5-foot-2 she had played basketball for many years, but was cut from the team at Martin High

Randi Miller is one of just five U.S. women to win an Olympic wrestling medal. John Sachs

School. Looking for another sport, and knowing she could avoid physical education class if she was playing a varsity sport, Miller joined the wrestling team and quickly became a starter. She caught on quickly, placing second at the Texas girls state high-school tournament and catching the attention of college recruiters. She wrestled two years at Neosho (Kansas) Community College and one year at MacMurray (Illnois) College before joining the U.S. Olympic Education Program at Northern Michigan University. She then moved to Colorado Springs to focus solely on wrestling at the U.S. Olympic Training Center.

In her early days on the Senior level, Miller learned from World champions Kristie Marano, Tricia Saunders and Iris Smith, and World medalist Katie Downing. "They taught me how to train, how to compete, how to cut weight. They taught me how to be a wrestler. They showed me the way. I had the inside track on how to be successful because of them."

Miller competed mostly at 72 kilograms/158 pounds and at 67 kilograms/147.5 pounds. With the 2008

Olympics coming up, she had a decision to make — go back up to 72 kilos or drop down to 63 kilograms/138.75 pounds. Her weight class of 67 kilograms was not an Olympic division. She decided to drop down to 63 kilograms in 2007 and knocked off Sara McMann in the finals of the Dave Schultz Memorial International in Colorado Springs. McMann came back to defeat Miller in the U.S. Open finals and went on to capture a bronze medal at the 2007 World Championships.

Even though she finished outside the top five at the 2007 World Team Trials, Miller's confidence did not waver. "Going into 2008, there was never, never, never, never any doubt that I could make the Olympic team. I believed in myself and I knew I could get it done. I just had to do what I needed to — good aggressive wrestling and staying in good position."

Miller did exactly that, knocking off McMann to win the 2008 U.S. Open and being named Outstanding Wrestler. She followed nearly two months later by sweeping McMann in two straight matches at the U.S. Olympic Trials in Las Vegas. "I obviously was happy to make the Olympic team, but still the job was only halfway done. My goal wasn't to be an Olympian — my goal was to be an Olympic champion."

The U.S. women's team was in California, making final preparations before leaving for the Olympics, when near-disaster struck for Miller. "We were playing a game and throwing a ball around, and I twisted my right ankle. I rolled it and it swelled up."

The good news was she still had a couple of weeks before her competition date. And when she took the mat for her first Olympic match, on August 17, 2008, her injured ankle was better. After the loss to Icho in the Olympic quarterfinals, Miller came back strong with a win in the repechage to earn a shot at Dugrenier in the bronze-medal match. Like Miller, Dugrenier had cut down to the Olympic weight class of 63 kilograms after previously competing at 67 kilograms. "I was embarrassed from the match I lost, and I was determined to come back strong. Martine had beaten me pretty handily before — it wasn't even close. But this time, I wanted to make sure I kept wrestling hard. I was going to keep going hard for six minutes. As soon as that first whistle blew, I was ready to compete."

The match went to a deciding third period and Miller came through to win an Olympic bronze. She jumped to her feet and unleashed a scream of joy before jumping into the arms of Coach Steiner. "I was pretty pumped. It kind of hit me later what it all meant, but during that moment I was just happy. I was sad too because I came to win gold, but I was happy to come back and win a

Randi Miller with her bronze medal at Beijing in 2008. John Sachs

bronze medal. And my mom was there, too. It was great to share that moment with her. It was pretty neat."

It was a huge win for Miller. Dugrenier went on to win three World titles and landed a spot in the United World Wrestling Hall of Fame.

Miller employed a more active and aggressive style in closing the Olympics with two straight victories. "I didn't even start wrestling like myself until the last two matches," she said in 2008. "I probably would have done better if I would have had that mentality to begin with."

Miller stepped away from competition after the 2008 Olympics. Four years later, while watching the webcast of the 2012 Olympics on her computer, Miller came to a realization — she missed the sport. She returned to competition after a five-year absence, making the 2014 U.S. World team at 69 kilograms/152 pounds. She placed third at the 2016 Olympic Trials.

Miller said she plans to keep competing and make a run at the 2020 Olympic Games. "I feel good and I know I am still competitive. It means a lot to be an Olympian. I made so many sacrifices to get to that level and I want to reach that level again. It was definitely worth all the hard work I did to get there in 2008. I'm the only African-American to have won an Olympic medal in women's wrestling. The whole experience in Beijing, it was pretty special and amazing."

During the time she has competed, Miller has seen the sport of women's wrestling grow on a number of different fronts. "Going from four to six Olympic weight classes was huge for the women. Now we have the same number of weights as freestyle and Greco. I think it's great to have more opportunities for the girls now. It shows more equality for the sport and that women's wrestling is being more accepted. The sport has grown a lot. It's awesome to see all the growth and progression of women's wrestling."

Miller said seeing an American woman win Olympic gold could have a widespread impact. "It would obviously mean a lot to finally see it happen. It would be so awesome to have it happen for the United States, and show that it is possible. When it does happen, we need to make sure people know who that person is. When we have an Olympic gold medalist, they need to get her name out there and keep it relevant for years to come."

Clarissa Chun (48 kilograms/105.5 pounds) and Ali Bernard (72 kilograms/158.5 pounds) also competed in bronze-medal matches at the 2008 Olympics, but both wrestlers fell short of medaling. Chun wrestled superbly in advancing to the semifinals. She held the lead late in her match against 2007 World champion Chiharu Icho of Japan before suffering a heartbreaking setback. She then lost by fall to Irini Merleni of Ukraine in the bronze-medal bout.

Meanwhile, Bernard lost to five-time World champion Kyoko Hamaguchi of Japan in her bronze-medal bout.

Marcie Van Dusen went 1-1 at the Olympics, falling to Colombia's Jackeline Renteria in the quarterfinals at 55 kilograms/121 pounds. Van Dusen emerged as a highly successful coach and leader within women's wrestling after her competitive career ended following the 2008 Olympics. She has served on USA Wrestling's Board of Directors along with the USA Wrestling Executive Committee and Athlete Advisory Committee and was named Woman of the Year in 2014 by USA Wrestling.

Van Dusen is the women's coach for the Titan Mercury Wrestling Club, one of the nation's premier clubs. The Titan women won three straight U.S. Open team titles from 2014-16. She was the first female to coach a women's college varsity wrestling team when she led Menlo College from 2010-12. Van Dusen was also a member of the 2007 U.S. World Team, a University World champion, a Pan American Games silver medalist and a Cadet World bronze medalist. In the 2008 Women's World Cup, she became the first wrestler to beat multiple Olympic and World champion Saori Yoshida of Japan in a Senior-level international match.

"I am very encouraged about women in wrestling," she said. "The opportunities are endless for women in all aspects of this sport, athletes, coaches, trainers and leaders. It continues to grow. A lot of things have come a long way, not just here in the United States but also internationally. It feels good to give back to the next generation and help build women's wrestling."

Two months after the Olympics, the World Championships were held in Tokyo.

Marcie Van Dusen now coaches the Titan Mercury Wrestling Club in California.

Chun rebounded from Beijing by becoming just the fifth American woman to win a World title. She relied on strong defense in defeating Jyldyz Eshimova of Kazakhstan 1-0, 1-0 at 48 kilograms, winning the first period from the defensive position in the clinch before countering and going behind the powerful 20-year-old Kazakhstan wrestler for the only takedown of the second period. "It's great to come back and win this after what happened at the Olympics," Chun said in 2008. "It feels great to be called a World champ, and I want more."

Teammate Tatiana Padilla won a bronze medal at 55 kilograms and added another in 2010. She eventually went on to excel in mixed martial arts and landed a spot in the Ultimate Fighting Championships.

Leading up to the Olympics, in March of 2008, coach Steiner said he started to notice a level of frustration with a number of the women's wrestlers at the Olympic Training Center in Colorado Springs. Much of the frustration stemmed from the style of Assistant Coach Vladislav "Izzy" Izboinikov, who grew up in Russia. Izboinikov was known as an excellent technician and a strict, hard-nosed, no-nonsense coach who was trained in the regimented Soviet system where athletes did exactly what they were told.

Olympic medalists Patricia Miranda, Sara McMann and Randi Miller were among 10 wrestlers who filed a grievance with USA Wrestling in July 2009, claiming gender discrimination and abusive behavior by national coaches that led to an exodus from the Olympic Training Center. They alleged USA Wrestling violated the Ted Stevens Olympic and Amateur Sports Act by not providing "equitable support and encouragement for participation by women."

Miranda wrote in the grievance that Steiner permitted behavior by Izboinikov that "continues to be tolerated and ignored." Miller claimed Izboinikov "antagonized me daily in the wrestling room. He would also publicly insult me and my work ethic."

Two-time World bronze medalist Katie Downing wrote that Izboinikov "acted like the biggest fan of an athlete one day, only to ignore, demean or disrespect them the next day. On top of that, he favored a small group of my teammates and mistreated the rest."

Steiner said he was "totally blindsided" when an article in the *Colorado Springs Gazette* on July 15, 2009 revealed that a grievance had been filed by the wrestlers. He met with Izboinikov a short time after and told him, "I need you to make some changes. But I don't know if you are capable of doing that."

"I want another shot," Izboinikov replied.

"This is your last shot," Steiner said.

Izboinikov did compromise and he remained as a U.S. assistant coach through the 2012 Olympics before becoming a school administrator in Colorado Springs. He was named Women's Coach of the Year by USA Wrestling in 2012.

"Coach Izzy came around and became better at communicating with the athletes," Steiner said. "I think some of the issues had to deal with cultural differences — he was used to doing things the way they did them in Russia. We worked together a lot better after 2009."

Steiner said he has tried to reach out to Miranda over the years, but they have not spoken since the grievance was filed. "And that really hurts — it still bothers me to this day. Patricia Miranda is a great human being who I have tremendous respect for. For her not to be a part of this program — one that she had a huge influence and huge impact on — is a shame. Maybe time will heal it.

"We lost a lot of athletes, and that hurt. I am hoping some of them come back and become involved in the sport again in some capacity. We need heroes around wrestling who can teach and guide and inspire the younger generation."

A rough year ended with the U.S. women failing to win a medal at the 2009 World Championships. Three wrestlers — Tatiana Padilla, Deanna Rix and Adeline Gray — each landed berths in bronze-medal matches but all three were defeated and finished fifth in their respective weight classes.

Wrestle Like A Girl

CHAPTER 9
Elena Pirozhkova

Elena Pirozhkova made a name for herself during the 2012 Olympic Games in London — but not quite in the way that anyone could have expected. She was there as U.S. First Lady Michelle Obama stopped by Team USA's London training facility in late July, walking down a long line while greeting American Olympians in a number of sports.

After watching each athlete hug the First Lady, Pirozhkova came up with a novel idea. "I wanted to do something different," she said. After hugging Mrs. Obama, Pirozhkova asked the First Lady a question: "Can I pick you up?"

A surprised Obama nervously replied, "Okay."

Pirozhkova then bent down and picked up the 5-11 Obama with both arms, cradling the First Lady in her arms.

The group of American athletes at the University of East London erupted in laughter and cheers.

"I think she was nervous," Pirozhkova said. "I went slow. I just picked her up. I wanted to ask her permission and she gave it. There was security all around. I will only meet her once, so I wanted to have a little fun with it."

A picture of the moment was captured by Clarissa Chun, posted on Twitter and was shown on websites all over the world. The White House later sent out its own image of Pirozhkova lifting Obama as its Photo of the Day and the story made international headlines — CNN aired a light-hearted story, complete with an interview and short feature on Pirozhkova.

The wrestler even had a name for the move she used to pick up Mrs. Obama: "It's a front body carry," she said with a laugh.

Pirozhkova gives a lift to Michelle Obama at the 2012 London Olympics. Sonya N. Hebert

After Elena put Obama back on her feet that day, the First Lady told Pirozhkova, "Oh, I'm a lot heavier than I seem."

Pirozhkova retorted, "No, I'm a lot stronger than I look."

Her opponents on the wrestling mat can attest to that. The Russian-born Pirozhkova has developed into one of the best female wrestlers in American history. She's won gold, silver, silver and bronze medals at the World Championships, and she's a two-time Olympian.

The road to those successes was a long and winding one for the wrestler, whose family (she was one of nine children) decided to leave the Soviet Union in 1990, shortly after the fall of the Berlin Wall. Pirozhkova's family lived in an industrial town in the Russian province of Siberia in an underdeveloped area accessed by dirt roads. They lived in a modest house without indoor plumbing and they had to bring coal inside to heat the house.

Pirozhkova's family were Pentecostal Christians. "A lot of the reason we left the Soviet Union was for religious freedom. My grandfather was a pastor and our family was very religious. It was difficult for us to live in that country because of the religion we practiced. My parents wanted to leave the Soviet Union to avoid religious persecution, and they wanted to move to a place where we would have an opportunity for a better life with more opportunities."

Leaving the country was not easy. Her father, Sergey, tried to obtain paperwork and was denied. He then told government officials his family was Jewish because he heard that might help their chances of being permitted to leave.

"He finally figured out he had to slip this lady an envelope of money to get out," Pirozhkova said.

Her father was in Moscow when he received the papers and documents he needed for his family to leave the country. He immediately sent a telegram back to the rest of his family in Siberia.

The message read: "Grab your stuff and go."

"We didn't even have time to say goodbye to a lot of our family and friends. We had to get out of there as quickly as we could."

Her mother, Tatyana, rounded up three-year-old Elena and her siblings and they boarded a train that took them from Siberia to Moscow, where they joined Sergey, and then fled to Vienna, Austria. After living there for a month, the family took a train to Italy, where they remained for four months before being permitted to travel to the United States. "My parents took a chance and it paid off for us. We got out of the Soviet Union just a couple of days before they closed the border. We were very fortunate we left when we did."

The family ended up settling in Greenfield, Massachusetts, a town of 18,000 people which would later attract a sizeable Russian community. "My parents were really strict when I was a kid. Disobeying your parents was like disobeying God. It was that scary. To go against their word, you wouldn't even think of it."

Pirozhkova received a rude awakening when it was time for her to start school. "I was still speaking only Russian when I went to kindergarten. My first day of school, I didn't know what to do. I didn't speak any English and I had no idea what was going on. That was a rough year."

Right before walking into school on her first day, she asked her brother a question in Russian. "What do I do if I have to go to the bathroom?" she asked.

"Just jump up and down," he said.

"Then they will know."

She was eager to learn, and by first grade was "speaking pretty good English." By fifth grade, she was taking advancing reading classes in English.

Her parents both worked a number of jobs to support the family. Her father had been an electrician in Russia. "Money was very, very tight," said Pirozhkova. "We grew up on welfare and lived on food stamps. My parents worked very hard, but it was still very difficult to get by. They did the best they could."

The family eventually expanded to nine children and everyone was called on to contribute to the family's well-being. "We were always doing something to pitch in," she said. "The whole family delivered the local newspaper — *The Recorder* — we had in Greenfield. We all had a paper route. We had to wake up very early in the morning and deliver papers in the dark. My toughest job was avoiding all of these dogs that were on my route. They were never on a leash, and I was so scared of them."

The family also owned 12 acres of land. "We all had work to do and chores to do. My dad would have us out digging a ditch, shoveling manure, mowing, planting something, or chopping wood. He didn't care if you were a girl or not. I really developed my work ethic when I was a kid. That has translated to my wrestling where I am the type of person who will just keep working until I get something done."

Pirozhkova's wrestling journey began in seventh grade, when her brother Viktor's team in Greenfield needed someone to compete in the 112-pound class. Viktor asked Elena to step on the scale to weigh herself, and talked her into joining the wrestling team. "It kind of started from there. I weighed 114 pounds, so I joined the team."

The first day she walked into practice, she witnessed something totally different from what she expected. "The only wrestling I had seen was the pro wrestling on TV, where guys were picking each other up and slamming them down in the World Wrestling Federation. There was no ring and no ropes in our wrestling room. Just a mat on the floor. The room was very small, and it was always freezing in there. The roof would leak and there would always be puddles on the mat. We only had one mat, and it was the hardest mat I've ever wrestled on. It was cracked, and it felt like a hard floor with a rug on it. It was uncomfortable and awkward. It hurt when I landed on the mat. And now, all of a sudden, I was up really close to a lot of boys."

After her first practice, her brother had a message for his little sister. "You should quit," he said, shaking his head. "I thought you were going to be more athletic."

That provided the motivation she

required. "When my brother told me that, it just made me determined to prove him wrong. I'm pretty stubborn. If you tell me I can't do something, I want to do it. I wanted to figure out how to wrestle. I loved how challenging it was and how much I had to push myself to become good at it."

Pirozhkova said early in her teenage years her relationship with her father began to evolve. "We became really close. We could talk about anything. He became a mentor."

She enjoyed a fair amount of success against boys at Greenfield High School, posting a winning record each year. At the club level she worked out with the New England All-Stars and Nieves Wrestling in Springfield. Aníbal Nieves, who wrestled in two Olympics, was her local coach.

Right after high school graduation, she gained the attention of USA Wrestling coaches while competing against girls at the 2005 Junior Nationals in Fargo, North Dakota. She finished third, earning a trip to the United States Olympic Training Center.

Following a second invite to training camp, USA Wrestling coaches made her an offer. "They asked me to move there. I wasn't that good. I didn't know why they wanted me."

The 18-year-old Pirozhkova accepted the offer and moved more than halfway across the country. She was mentored

Elena Pirozhkova takes it to her opponent from China. John Sachs

by her fellow Russian, coach Izboinikov during much of her time in Colorado Springs.

In 2008, she made her first World Team, beginning a long run of consecutive appearances at the event. The same man who had driven away so many other talented American wrestlers had a very different impact on Pirozhkova. "Izzy made my career. Without him, I wouldn't be where I am now. He found me and molded me into the athlete I am. He was the one who brought me to Colorado Springs. That changed everything for me. He taught me so much technique, but he also taught me the mental side of the sport. He was a great mentor who invested so much time into me. He really understood what I was going through."

It was fitting that Pirozhkova enjoyed a breakthrough on the Senior level in her homeland, at the 2010 World Championships in Moscow. With Coach Izzy in her corner, Pirozhkova won a silver medal at 63 kilograms/138.75 pounds, finishing second to Japanese legend Kaori Icho, who had two Olympic gold medals in her locker. "It was the first time I had been back to Russia since my family left when I was three. It was pretty cool to have an opportunity to go back there. It helped me understand my heritage more and see a little bit of what their culture was like. It made that first one extra special."

When she returned home with her first World medal, she showed it to her father. "Why didn't you get first?" was his matter-of-fact response.

"My parents expected me to be the best at whatever I did. Not that my dad wasn't proud of me. They just encouraged us to work hard to be the best." For her efforts, Pirozhkova was named the 2010 USA Wrestling Women's Wrestler of the Year.

Heartbreak struck less than two months before the 2011 World Championships when Sergey died after battling with cirrhosis of the liver. He was 54 years old. "My dad had been sick for a while. He had almost died three years before that."

During the final week of his life, Sergey was so ill he couldn't speak. "We knew the end was coming, but it was still hard no matter what," she said.

Despite losing three weeks of training, Pirozhkova managed to place fifth at the 2011 Worlds in Istanbul, Turkey. She won her first four matches before falling to Icho in the semifinals. She then dropped her bronze-medal match to finish 4-2 on a long, grueling day where she wrestled six matches. "I was so worn down from everything that had happened. I was so tired in my last match, I just wanted to lay down and take a nap. But I learned from that experience. I train a lot smarter now and I've had good performances at the Worlds since then."

Even after a rough 2011, Pirozhkova came into the 2012 London Games confident she could make a run at a medal, which made the disappointment of losing in the first round and failing to medal even harder to take (see chapter 10). "I'm still not exactly sure what happened at the Olympics. I anted to wrestle and I was excited to compete, but when I got out there I couldn't move and I couldn't breathe. I didn't feel good at all and it just didn't feel right. It was rough."

Less than two months after the Olympic disappointment, Pirozhkova walked onto the mat to face Bulgaria's Taybe Yusein in the gold-medal match at the 2012 World Championships in Edmonton, Canada. Pirozhkova won the first period 2-1, but dropped the second period 5-2 to the 2011 Junior World champion.

She then won the third and decisive period 1-0 to become the champion, countering a leg attack and spinning behind Yusein for the eventual winning takedown with just under a minute left. "I came in here really focused," she said after the win. "I really got after it and wrestled aggressively. I scrapped and I fought, and I got it done."

Her only regret was that father Sergey was not there to see it. "He would have been proud."

Pirozhkova followed by earning a World bronze medal in 2013 and a silver in 2014. "Elena has come a long way and that's a credit to her perseverance," coach Steiner said. "She came to the Olympic Training Center when she was very young. Elena just bought in. She was just a sponge — she listened and she was eager to learn. She wasn't the greatest athlete in the world, but she slowly kept building and progressing. She's competed for over 10 years at a very elite level and that's pretty impressive. A lot of credit for Elena's success goes to Coach Izzy. He got her on the right path and taught her so much."

Pirozhkova's list of accomplishments on the wrestling mat are among the most impressive in the sport. Besides being a World champion and a two-time Olympian, she has...

• Wrestled on nine consecutive U.S. World or Olympic national teams (2008-2016)

• Won seven straight U.S. Open titles (2009-2015)

• Won the Pan-American championships four times

The Olympic loss from 2012 still wrankles, though she uses it as a force for good. "It really motivates and it really pushes me — I still think about it a lot. I have matured a lot since then and I'm a better wrestler now."

Pirozhkova now trains under Valentin Kalika, who also grew up in the former Soviet Union. They met in 2014, just a few hours after Pirozhkova had won the U.S. Open in Las Vegas. Kalika had been working with top young men's freestyle standout Aaron Pico in California.

Shortly after they started talking in English, Kalika had a question for Pirozhkova.

"Do you speak Russian?" he said.

"Yes, I do," she replied.

"So we sat down, had a beer and ordered a pizza, and just started talking," Pirozhkova said. "Within the first 10 minutes, I asked him if I could go out to California and have him work with me as a coach. I went there for a month and I knew right away he was going to be the missing piece to help get me ready for the 2016 Olympics in Rio."

A few months later, Kalika was in Pirozhkova's corner when she won a silver medal at the 2014 World Championships in Tashkent, Uzbekistan. "I connected with Valentin. I need a good relationship with my coach, on and off the mat, and I feel like we have that. He understands what I need as an athlete."

Kalika spent the first month he coached Pirozhkova studying and analyzing her style of wrestling. "He didn't try to change my wrestling style. He just tried to build and expand on it, and refine what I was already doing. He tried to enhance parts that I was missing."

There were times when Pirozhkova was reluctant to try a technique that Kalika thought she might incorporate into her vast wrestling arsenal. "Valentin would drive me crazy sometimes. He would have me work on things over and over, and I just couldn't see it working for me. But sometimes learning and developing a new technique takes a while. There are things he's taught me that I never dreamed would work in a match, but they are actually working for me now. I'm so grateful to have him in my corner now. I trust him and I believe in what he's telling me."

In an interview prior to the 2016 Olympics, Pirozhkova talked about her preparations and her goals. "I have a new technical coach, a new strength coach, a dietitian and I think the results are kind of speaking for themselves. I want the gold; nothing less than the gold is going to make me happy right now."

Elena Pirozhkova represented the U.S. on nine consecutive World or Olympic national teams. Jen Gutches

CHAPTER 10
London: The 2012 Olympics

Clarissa Kyoko Mei Ling Chun was born in Kapolei, Hawaii, just outside Honolulu — her mother, Gail, is Japanese-American and her father, Bryan, is Chinese-American. She grew up competing in swimming, water polo and judo and didn't take up wrestling until she was 16. She was a five-time junior national champion in judo, which caught the attention of her high school coaches. Girls' wrestling was sanctioned scholastically at the high school level in Hawaii in the mid-1990s, and Roosevelt High School coach Bryan Aspera encouraged Chun to try out for wrestling. "I wasn't winning in swimming, so I tried wrestling. That's basically how it all started for me."

Chun caught on quickly, relying heavily on her arsenal of judo moves and throws to win back-to-back Hawaii state wrestling championships in 1998 and 1999.

She entered the 1999 USGWA High School Nationals in Michigan and placed third, losing in the semifinals to Mary Kelly, who became a Cadet World champion later that year before winning two Junior World medals. Kelly made a U.S. Senior World Team in 2006, defeating Chun in a wrestle-off.

"Mary was the first girl who beat me," Chun said. "It was a really close match and I was pretty upset that I lost."

Chun's performance impressed the attention of coaches at Missouri Valley College. "I had no idea there was anything after high school wrestling. Once they offered a scholarship, I decided to give it a shot. Going from Honolulu, Hawaii to Marshall, Missouri was a pretty big culture shock. But there were four other girls and two guys from Hawaii who went to Missouri Valley for

Clarissa Chun was a two-time high school wrestling champion in Hawaii. Tony Rotundo

wrestling. And there was one guy there from my high school who played on the football team. It was a big change, but we had a group of us that we knew and that helped out quite a bit."

Chun was just learning how to wrestle freestyle when she made both the U.S. Senior and Junior World Teams in 2000. She had only turned 19 when she stepped on the mat for the 2000 Senior World Championships in Sofia, Bulgaria. She was thrown right into the fire and lost by fall to wrestlers from Russia and Mexico at 46 kilograms/101.25 pounds. "I was a little overwhelmed, and in awe of it all. I remember Kristie [Marano] winning a World title and wrestling really well. I remember not wrestling well at all. I was a deer in the headlights and thinking, 'What I am doing here?' It was a separate Worlds, with just women and no guys. I felt very inexperienced. I felt so lost out there. I honestly didn't think I belonged out there and it showed."

Chun came back in 2001 to place fifth at the Junior Worlds and began placing consistently in Senior-level events. She left Missouri Valley after three years when it was announced in 2002 they were starting a program for women's wrestling at the U.S. Olympic Training Center.

Chun placed second to Patricia Miranda at the first Olympic Trials for women's wrestling in 2004 at the RCA Dome in Indianapolis, Indiana. It was a portent of things to come in the lightest women's weight class of 48 kilograms/105.5 pounds.

"There were a lot of girls who were older and more experienced than me. I think a lot of it was mental and I just wasn't able to break through. Patricia was big and strong, and she trained hard. I probably gave her too much respect. After that loss, I felt I was wasting my time. I thought to myself, 'What am I doing?' I felt like I had the ability physically. I had the skill and the work ethic to do it. I just didn't believe in myself the way I needed to."

Chun started working more closely with Keith Wilson, a tough, hard-nosed character who coached the women's athletes in the Sunkist Kids Wrestling Club.

Under Wilson's guidance, Chun became stronger mentally and physically. Undersized for her weight class of 48 kilograms/105.5 pounds, the 4-foot-11 Chun used a strength-training program to match up better with the bigger girls in her division. She was no longer being overpowered by bigger opponents. "In 2008, everything eventually started to click for me. I worked with Coach Wilson and he helped me improve on the little things I needed to do to win those close matches. We worked very hard in every area I needed. And he helped me a lot on the mental side. He had me believing I could beat anybody."

Chun finished a disappointing fourth at the 2008 U.S. Open, but a semifinal loss to Miranda in that tournament changed her perspective. Chun turned to Wilson while walking off the mat and told him, "I'm never going to lose to her again."

"That match wasn't controversial or anything, I just finally had a feeling I could beat her," Chun said. "That month and a half before the Olympic Trials, I trained hard. I was ready to go when we wrestled again."

Six weeks later, Chun and Miranda went head to head in Las Vegas, with a berth in the 2008 Olympics at stake. Chun took two straight matches from the 2004 Olympic bronze medalist and advanced to the Beijing Olympics.

Chun powered in for a double-leg takedown to punctuate her series sweep

Clarissa Chun with her Olympic bronze medal in 2012. John Sachs

over Miranda at 48 kilograms/105.5 pounds. "It was an incredible feeling to make my first Olympic team. Pure joy and pure happiness."

Chun wasn't considered one of the favorites entering the 2008 Olympics. When the brackets came out the night before she competed, Chun didn't want to know her draw. "I never looked at the brackets the night before. I didn't want to know something that would keep me up at night."

The next morning, Steiner sought out Chun right away. "You ready to see your draw?" he asked.

"Yes, I'm ready," Chun replied.

"You have Sweden," Steiner said.

That meant taking on young star Sofia Mattsson, who had already beaten Chun three times that season. "I was ready to go. I had a goal of winning the Olympics, and I was ready."

Chun came out determined and earned a clutch 2-1, 4-1 win over Mattsson, who won a World title the next year. Chun followed by sweeping France's Vanessa Boubryemm 6-1, 2-1 in the quarterfinals. "I was feeling great," Chun said, "and confident."

Next up was a semifinal bout against reigning World champion Chiharu Icho of Japan. Chun had the lead in the match's final minute before Icho rallied for a victory.

"That was a really tough match," Chun said. "I had a flood of emotions — I was pissed off, I was frustrated and I was crying because I didn't make the finals. I was so disappointed with the loss to Japan. I wanted to wrestle [Canada's] Carol Huynh in the finals."

Chun tried to regroup, but lost to Irini Merleni in the bronze-medal match. "I wanted to go back out there and win a medal. It just didn't happen."

Chun took some time off until the World Championships in Tokyo in October. "I wasn't in the greatest shape when they had the trials, plus I had been sick. But I really wanted to go to Japan. And I was still bitter and upset about what happened at the Olympics."

Chun started strong, winning her first two matches by fall. She then earned a hard-fought, three-period win over World bronze medalist Makiko Sakamoto of Japan in the semifinals before defeating Jyldyz Eshimova-Turtbayeva of Kazakhstan 1-0, 1-0 in the finals.

The large group of Japanese fans stood and cheered as Chun's hand was raised in victory.

Less than two months after a tough finish at the Olympics, Chun was a World champion. A large group of Japanese photographers and reporters were matside to chronicle her triumph, and a press conference with a large group of Japanese media was held. "I am part Japanese, so it was really special to win it in Tokyo."

Chun followed through on an earlier commitment by teaching English in Japan, working with elementary school students.

She returned to competition and followed by making World teams in 2009 and 2011, but she came up short of medaling, slowed by injuries. "I was thinking about being done with wrestling in 2008. But because of that semifinal loss at the Olympics, I felt like I wasn't completely done competing."

Chun underlined this point when she made her second Olympic team in 2012, outlasting Alyssa Lampe, who would go on to win two World bronze medals for the U.S. Lampe was a gritty, hard-nosed competitor — all three matches went the full three periods.

Chun rallied for an 0-2, 1-0, 3-1 victory in the first match of the best-of-3 series then came out strong in Match 2, rolling to a 7-0 win in the first period. But Lampe regrouped to win the final two periods 2-2, 5-2 to force a deciding third match.

A distraught Chun sat down near the edge of the mat, shaking her head in frustration. "Lampe's a tough, tough competitor — we had some really intense matches. She wasn't going to give me anything. Wrestling her made me better and made me stronger, physically and mentally."

Chun regrouped and dug down in the third match, taking the first period 2-0 before Lampe won the second 2-2 on criteria.

The 2012 Olympic berth would come down to one last two-minute period, which Chun won 4-1. "It took everything I had to beat Lampe — everything."

But the battle wasn't over for Chun, who endured a difficult time after making the Olympic team. She and Wilson, her long-time coach, parted ways just before the 2012 Games. "I was breaking down and crying every day in practice. I had all of these emotions and questions. I was struggling mentally."

Shortly before the U.S. team departed for London, Chun traveled to San Jose, California to attend a seminar called "Unleash the Power Within," led by motivational speaker Tony Robbins. "It was refreshing and rejuvenating. He was trying to get your mind to think anything is possible."

Which included walking across a bed of hot coals.

"It was what I went for, to make some changes. I needed to shake some things up. So I walked across hot coals on the first day of the seminar, and I got blisters on both of my feet."

Chun's coaches quickly figured out what had happened when they saw her hobbling around after she returned to Colorado. "You ding dong!" Assistant Coach Vladislav Izboinikov told Chun. "What were you thinking?"

Elena Pirozhkova was upset in the first round of the 2012 Olympics. John Sachs

Kelsey Campbell surprises Helen Maroulis at the 2012 Olympic Trials. Brooke Zumas

Coach Terry Steiner simply shook his head in frustration.

"In the beginning, I was in a lot of pain," Chun said. "I had a blister on the ball of my right foot. It was in a real sensitive place where I push off and drive off on that foot. I was just glad I had some time to heal. I knew I had to show up and get ready to compete."

The blister was still bothering Chun when she arrived in London. "But it finally got better. It literally healed just in time to compete in the Olympics."

Chun followed the same routine she had in 2008 — she didn't want to see her draw until the day of the competition.

She woke up that morning and Steiner had his question ready: "You want to know who you got?"

"Okay," Chun responded.

"You've got China first round. Do you want to watch video on her?"

"I'm not much of a video watcher," Chun said. "But Terry showed me what her tendencies were and what her go-to move was. We came up with a game plan and a strategy to make sure we didn't get out of position."

Chun came out strong to earn a 5-0, 1-0 win over World bronze medalist Shasha Zhou before falling to World champion Maria Stadnyk of Azerbaijan in the quarterfinals.

"I started out well, but I didn't shift gears for Stadnyk. Her motion was a lot different. I was not prepared for that."

Chun stormed back to pin Poland's Iwona Matkowska of Poland to set the stage for a rematch with Irina Merleni in the bronze-medal bout.

Merleni had pinned Chun in the bronze-medal bout at the 2008 Olympics. But Chun was not going to be denied this time, winning 1-0, 3-0. She fired in for a clutch double-leg takedown and finished with just three seconds left to take the first period 1-0 at 48 kilograms/105.5 pounds. Chun then delivered with a huge three-point arm throw late in the second period en route to earning the bronze. "I remembered the feeling of losing to Merleni in 2008. She was very physical and very powerful, but I went out there and wrestled my match. I had a totally different mindset this time. I threw her at the end of the match when she was trying to score. I wasn't going to give her anything."

The sellout crowd of 6,500 fans stood and cheered as Chun ran around the mat holding an American flag above her head. "I was so happy. My family and friends from Hawaii were there. It almost made up for what happened in Beijing. I wish I would've been on top of the podium and getting that gold medal, but it was still a great experience seeing the American flag going up during the medal ceremony. We needed that. I was the first U.S. medalist in wrestling that year. It was awesome to be able to do that for my country."

Steiner credited Chun's resiliency in London. "Clarissa had a great tournament. That girl from China was tough, and then she had a good win over a strong opponent from Poland. And then to beat a wrestler the caliber of Merleni, that was a huge win. She wrestled perfectly in that last match."

"I learned from Beijing — I didn't get in the emotional rollercoaster ride," Chun said. "I stayed calm, cool and collected. I'm so grateful for every opportunity I have to step on the mat. Gold is what I strive for, but I'm happy with the bronze. For me, it was about finishing strong. That's the difference I made from Beijing when I lost in the semis. I was a nervous wreck after I lost in 2008."

"Clarissa's gone through a lot of tough times," Steiner said that day. "To hold things together and believe she could do it here is impressive. She's just an unbelievable athlete and a super human being on top of that. I'm so happy for her."

Chun continued to wrestle at a high level through the next Olympic cycle. She won the final two matches of her career at age 34 to place third in a very strong weight class at the 2016 Olympic Trials in Iowa City, Iowa.

"I'm always pretty hard on myself and pretty critical of my performances," Chun said that day. "I wish I could've done more and could've wrestled better. I gave it everything I had. I still love the sport. No matter how old you are, you can still have that drive to be the best and the motivation to be successful. Wrestling's such a great sport."

Chun underwent three shoulder surgeries, two on her knee and one on her elbow during a storied career. "I have no regrets — I wouldn't have done it any other way. The sport of wrestling has really shaped the person who I am today."

Chun is one of just three U.S. women to make two Olympic wrestling teams and is one of five to win an Olympic medal. "It's awesome to be part of that group. It's tough to win an Olympic medal."

"Clarissa had a very good career," Steiner said. "She's one of our great champions. She won a lot of big matches in her career. She meant so much to our program and she did a lot for women's wrestling."

Elena Pirozhkova, considered a medal contender, dropped her first Olympic match in three periods to 2012 European runner-up Anastasija Grigorjeva of Latvia. Pirozhkova won the first period 2-0 on a pair of takedowns before the Latvian prevailed 5-0, 2-0 in the final two periods at 63 kilograms/138.75 pounds.

"She had a good strategy," Pirozhkova said. "She kept pressuring me and trying to wear me out. I felt pretty confident going into the match. I had studied her and had a good game plan. But it was a higher pace than I expected. I couldn't sustain the match pace. I have a lot more conditioning I need to work on."

Pirozhkova was eliminated when Grigorjeva fell short of reaching the finals. "We didn't find a way to slow her down and raise our level up," Assistant Coach Izboinikov said. "We got exposed out there. We have to be able to wrestle at a higher pace and get in the fight. Unfortunately, we weren't able to do that today."

Pirozhkova had defeated Adeline Gray to make the 2012 Olympic team. Gray had cut down a weight after winning a World bronze medal in 2011 at 67 kilograms/147.5 pounds.

Kelsey Campbell (55 kilograms/121 pounds) and Ali Bernard (72 kilograms/158.5 pounds) also came up short in London. Campbell (who had made the team after knocking off favored Helen Maroulis in the trials) had a brutal draw, falling 1-0, 1-0 to Saori Yoshida of Japan, who went on to win her third straight Olympic gold. She then lost to World champion Yulia Ratkevich of Azerbaijan in the wrestlebacks. Four years later, Campbell once again won the Olympic Trials at 58 kilograms/128 pounds; however, she was unable to qualify the weight for the U.S. team.

Meanwhile, Bernard lost in the first round to Sweden's Jenny Fransson, who would earn a World title later that year. Bernard had lost to past World team member Stephany Lee in the finals of the 2012 trials, but Lee failed a post-match drug test and Bernard took her place on the team.

Wrestle Like A Girl   **119**

CHAPTER 11
The fight to stay in the Games

Cellular phones were buzzing, dinging and ringing before the sun came up in many parts of the country. The news spread quickly across the United States in the early morning hours of February 12, 2013. The International Olympic Committee Executive Board was voting that day in Switzerland to recommend that one core sport be removed from the Olympic Games program for 2020 so that a new sport could be added.

In a stunning, puzzling and controversial decision, the 15-member IOC Executive Board voted to recommend that wrestling be removed. There was shock and outrage worldwide at the IOC vote, especially with wrestling's long and storied place as one of the original Olympic sports.

The good news was that there still was hope. Immediately after the initial vote, the IOC was being heavily criticized around the world for its surprise decision.

People around the globe, in and out of the sport, began to rally behind wrestling. On May 29, in St. Petersburg, Russia, wrestling took its first dramatic step in retaining its spot in the Olympics. The IOC had invited wrestling, plus seven other sports, to make a presentation to their Executive Board that afternoon.

After the presentations, five of those eight sports would be eliminated by a vote of the Executive Board from further consideration of being the one sport added to the 2020 and 2024 Olympics. The presentations were made and a vote was taken. The same IOC Executive Board that recommended wrestling be removed from the Olympic program in February chose wrestling, baseball/softball and squash to be shortlisted for

Victoria Anthony was one of several U.S. women competing in the United 4 Wrestling event in Los Angeles in May, 2013. Tony Rotundo

the one open spot.

The final vote to add one sport for the 2020 and 2024 Olympic Games would be made at the IOC General Assembly in September.

Being one of three finalists showed that wrestling wasn't going away quietly. And many Olympic observers now considered wrestling the favorite to be added to 2020 and 2024.

Female wrestlers played an integral role in the two important presentations to the IOC that kept wrestling in the Olympics. Canada's Carol Huynh and France's Lise Legrand were chosen as part of the five-person presentation team. Huynh was a 2008 Olympic gold medalist for Canada while Legrand was a 2004 Olympic medalist for France.

Another key component in the fight to keep wrestling in the Olympics was the involvement of members of the early women's World teams for the United States. A reunion honoring what USA Wrestling called The Pioneers of Women's Wrestling was held in April, 2013 in Las Vegas during the U.S. Open.

A large group of women, including Tricia Saunders, Afsoon Roshanzamir and Marie Ziegler, took part in the festivities.

"Terry Steiner called me and asked me to get back involved when they were trying to drop wrestling from the Olympics in 2013," said Roshanzamir. "I started becoming much more involved in the sport again during the 2013 Olympic fight after the IOC threatened to remove wrestling from the Olympic program."

She was among those who took part in a Saving Wrestling event at Niagara Falls, Canada in May that was called the Battle at the Falls. Women's teams from Canada, the U.S. and the Ukraine competed. "Women's wrestling played a huge role in keeping the sport in the Olympic program, and we were able to gain more Olympic weight classes because of it. I returned to a more active role with the women's program during this Olympic quad, from 2013-16, going on overseas tours as a coach and in a medical capacity."

She served as a World team coach in 2014 in Tashkent, Uzbekistan, where the team finished third.

One of the top events for Saving Wrestling in the Olympics was the United 4 Wrestling international matches held in Los Angeles in May, 2013. This event pitted top U.S. wres-

The U.S., Canadian and Ukrainian women's

tlers against Olympic wrestling opponents from Russia and Canada. Elena Pirozhkova and Brittany Roberts were the two U.S. women to win their bout.

Later that summer, an outdoors wrestling tournament was staged at the site of the original Olympic Games in Athens, Greece. Among the athletes who took part was women's free-

teams at a Saving Wrestling event at Niagara Falls in 2013. Brock University

style standout Helen Maroulis, whose father is from Greece. Maroulis, Alyssa Lampe, Elena Pirozhkova and Tamyra Mensah all made the tournament finals but only Lampe at 48 kilograms emerged as a champion. The others lost to their Russian opponents and settled for silver medals.

Another key component in wrestling's quest to stay in the Olympic Games was the change in the structure of weight classes. Wrestling competed in a total of 18 weight classes at the 2012 Olympics, but only four divisions included women. There were seven weight classes apiece for men's freestyle and Greco-Roman, but only four women's freestyle classes at the 2004, 2008 and 2012 Games.

Adding more weight classes would not only present more opportunities for women, but demonstrated that international wrestling was making a stronger commitment to female athletes.

Showing more equity for women would address criticisms that the IOC and others had of wrestling in the past where the leadership was almost exclusively male at the international level.

A proposal was made to add two weight classes for the women at the Olympics while taking one away from both men's freestyle and Greco-Roman. The move to 6-6-6 was approved in June 2013. It was voted to go into effect at the 2016 Games in Rio de Janeiro.

"Going to 6-6-6 is exciting," Adeline Gray said in 2013. "Having those two extra spots at the Olympics will make a big difference. It was always difficult trying to squeeze women wrestlers into just four weight classes. It was very difficult to wrestle at your optimum weight. Many girls were caught between weight classes when going for the Olympics."

Gray said she hated seeing the men lose weight classes, but understood the role of women in the Olympic fight. "I agree with the people who say that women can be the ones to save the sport of wrestling," she said in 2013.

Kyle Dake, a four-time NCAA champion, also endorsed the expanded role that women were gaining in the sport. "Anyone can be a wrestler," he said. "You don't have to be a male. That's a great thing about our sport."

And as wrestling legend Dan Gable, who played a significant role in 2013, astutely pointed out, "6-6-6 is better than 0-0-0."

The push by United World Wrestling president Nenad Lalovic and the international wrestling federation looked to be paying off as wrestling made its final push late in the summer of 2013 to stay in the Olympics. And finally, 208 days after the first IOC vote, three sports made their final pitch to the IOC General Assembly on a September afternoon in Buenos Aires, Argentina.

Huynh and LeGrand gave their presentations again on behalf of wrestling, along with Lalovic, former U.S. Olympic Committee leader Jim Scherr and Olympic gold medalist Daniel Igali. Baseball/softball and squash also made presentations before representatives of the three sports gathered for the results of the vote.

At USA Wrestling headquarters in Colorado Springs, Colorado, a large group of women's wrestlers had gathered to watch the final presentations and the IOC vote on a large flat-screen television. The room became quiet when IOC president Jacques Rogge stepped to the podium to announce the results of the vote.

Wrestling would stay in the Games.

The room erupted in cheers, and hugs and high-fives were exchanged among the smiling athletes in the room.

Women's wrestling demonstrated its importance to the Olympic world in 2013, making a positive impact that will be felt for many years to come.

"It was a very difficult and trying year for a lot of people in wrestling, but it was also a very exciting year for the sport as well," said Roshanzamir. "The sport became considerably better, the leadership improved tremendously on the international level and there became even more opportunities for women in wrestling.

"There are still ways that the sport of women's wrestling can advance and evolve, but we have come so far when you consider what it was like in 1989. It's been amazing to see."

CHAPTER 12
Leigh Jaynes

There were times when Leigh Jaynes wondered if this day would ever come. And if Father Time had indeed passed her by. She was 34 years old, a dinosaur of sorts in the world of women's wrestling where many of her contemporaries had long since retired to start families and careers of their own.

Jaynes had made a World team in women's freestyle wrestling in 2007 and 2012. She lost early in both tournaments and fell short of the medal podium.

After that, she married Olympic Greco-Roman wrestler Ben Provisor and gave birth to a daughter, Evelyn, in 2013. The new mother wanted to return to the mat but needed to lose 50 pounds after her pregnancy to drop down to her competition weight class.

But Jaynes is a fighter, and she has a knack for proving people wrong.

She continued to train and the weight started to come off. She returned to the mat and, after some early struggles, started to win matches again.

And her big day on the wrestling mat finally arrived. It was the evening of September 12, 2015 when Jaynes stepped onto the elevated platform for the biggest match of her life. A packed house of pro-American fans was on hand at the World Wrestling Championships to watch her take the mat for her bronze-medal match at 60 kilograms/132 pounds.

It had been a long, trying and difficult journey to arrive at this point for Jaynes.

It's only fitting that her introduction into the sport came in an unconventional manner. Jaynes, then 17 years old, was on a rock-climbing trip with a youth group that included Brian Bowker, a high-school coach in her native New

Leigh Jaynes endured a tough road on the way to building a wrestling career. Jim Gutches

Jersey. Jaynes made a sarcastic remark to Bowker and the wrestling coach at Rancocas Valley Regional High School immediately fired back. "You think you are bad, but you wouldn't last two weeks in the wrestling room. I don't think you're tough enough."

Shortly after that, Jaynes ran into Bowker in the cafeteria at school. "Were you serious about me coming out for wrestling?" she said.

"Absolutely," he said. "Come on out."

Lasting two weeks in the wrestling room was nothing compared to what Jaynes had already been through during a tumultuous and stress-filled childhood. She grew up in Mount Holly, just outside Philadelphia. Her father, Clayton Jaynes, had served in the Vietnam War and struggled with post-traumatic stress disorder and drug addiction. That took its toll on Leigh's mother, Karen Williams, who left her husband soon after Leigh was born.

"It was definitely a messed-up situation," Jaynes said. At age 11, she was sent to a rehabilitation center because social workers believed she was using drugs, though she denied it. After 56 days in the rehab center, she was transferred to the psychiatric ward of a hospital.

"They sent me to the psych ward because I wouldn't admit I was using drugs. I wasn't going to admit to something I didn't do. I was telling the truth and I stayed true to myself. None of it made sense. I was a straight-A student and I was in the band, and I was doing really well in school. I wouldn't accept these stigmas they were putting on me."

Her mother struggled financially, trying to raise Jaynes and her brother, Michael. She eventually turned to the state for help, signing up for a temporary child placement to find care for the children. "My mom was having a hard time. It was a stressful situation and a really hostile environment."

Jaynes was 12 when her mother relinquished custody of her. She was sent to live in a group home with seven other girls with troubled backgrounds. She was there until she turned 16. "It was a nightmare — all of the girls were pretty messed up when they got there. Some were worse than others. It was rough. I never really had a chance to grow up in a normal home environment."

Jaynes endured her share of negative comments during that time, including many that were racist. "I was a child of mixed race, and in their eyes, I was never white enough or never black enough. That is the age when kids do a lot of bullying. Some of the kids could be unbelievably cruel. I was lucky, because I'm strong and I'm resilient."

When she turned 16, Jaynes made a decision — she was ready to be on her own. She applied to be an emancipated minor, meaning she would be released

Leigh Jaynes with daughter Evelyn. Jen Gutches

from the legal authority of her parents. "I believed I could do better on my own than in this stressful environment I was in with all these crazy people. I had some serious emotional damage and didn't fit in anywhere. I was a social outcast. I just wanted to be normal."

Her petition for emancipation was granted by the state of New Jersey, but it was still a struggle for her. She lived off and on with friends and families, but at times she had trouble finding a place to stay. "I slept in my car. I slept on a bench. I stayed in a hotel. I was pretty much on my own, and I got into the habit of running away from situations that were too hard for me to handle. There were a lot of times where I had a trash bag with all of my stuff in it, and I would just go from place to place."

But then Jaynes found wrestling, and eventually found a home in a grueling, demanding sport that takes a tremendous amount of dedication and sacrifice. She won over the boys on her high-school team with her work ethic and determination. "I was so horrible in the beginning — I was the worst wrestler ever. But I finally found a place where I fit in. I loved it. I took my hits, but when I got knocked down I got back up. I really needed that in my life. It was kind of poetic because it was kind of the story of my life."

Wrestling was a breeze for Jaynes compared to what she had been through. During her first match, she scored a takedown before being hit in the mouth with an elbow. Even though one of her teeth had been knocked out, she continued to wrestle. She was winning and didn't want to stop.

Following her senior season, Jaynes placed sixth at a national tournament in Flint, Michigan while competing against girls for the first time. She thought she might be done competing, but then a call came with an offer to wrestle for a college program at Missouri Valley. "They offered me a scholarship. I gave my friend $100 to drive me to Missouri. She got the short end of the stick because Missouri was a lot further away from New Jersey than I thought it was."

Missouri Valley was a powerhouse program and was ranked No. 1 in the country. Jaynes graduated from Missouri Valley, earning bachelor's and master's degrees. She eventually joined the U.S. Army and moved to Colorado Springs to train at the U.S. Olympic Training Center, competing for the Army's World Class Athlete Program.

Jaynes became a force on the Senior level and made her first World team in 2007. Her first match at the 2007 World Championships was against two-time returning World champion Ayako Shoda of Japan and she lost a close match in the first round at 59 kilograms/130 pounds. "I actually scored first, but she came back to take the lead and then held on to beat me. I showed her too much respect. I worked on the mindset to have the mentality to win no matter who I am wrestling against."

Jaynes placed fourth at the 2008 Olympic Trials and was considered a top contender at the 2012 trials after placing second at the U.S. Open. But she failed to make weight after trying to cut down to 55 kilograms/121 pounds. "I thought I was going to make the Olympic team. I thought it was my time. It was tough, but I've been through a lot in my life. When I experience a setback, I can bounce back and not let it keep me down."

Shortly after the 2012 Olympics, Jaynes moved back up to her preferred weight class of 59 kilograms and made her second World team. But she suffered another first-round loss and fell short of medaling once again.

Those setbacks weighed heavily. "Part of me felt like I didn't deserve it. I think a lot of my background and my past had to do with whether I was worthy or not. There were just these issues that were underlying. I felt like I had to take a step back and really, really deal with it and accept it, and do whatever I had to do to move forward."

Jaynes called her father in 2015, forgiving him and welcoming him into her family. She said her mother also is part of her life now.

After the birth of her daughter, Jaynes was determined to work her way back into shape and take one last shot at achieving her wrestling dreams. "It was really, really hard when I started training again. There were days when it hurt so bad, I didn't want to get out of bed. But I kept pushing and kept working. I couldn't see myself giving up."

She struggled in 2014, dropping match after match in her return to the mat. "I spent that whole year losing matches. It was pretty bad at times. I could've just hung it up, and just been a mommy and taken care of my daughter. But I wanted to wrestle and be a mom, and you know what, you can do both."

She returned to form at the 2015 U.S. Open, earning a title at 60 kilograms/132 pounds, and followed that up by sweeping talented young wrestler Jennifer Page in a pair of wild, high-scoring bouts to make her third World team.

Just a few days later, Jaynes was vacationing on a camping trip in the Colorado mountains with her husband and daughter when their Subaru Outback was hit by an Acura SUV at an intersection. "That SUV came flying over a hill," Jaynes said. "They were going about 60 miles per hour when it hit us."

The impact of the crash rolled the Subaru over and the vehicle came to rest on the driver's side. Jaynes suffered the worst of the crash since she was sitting on the passenger's side, where the impact occurred. "I suffered a severe concussion. I was in shock and I was disoriented. It was a potentially fatal accident. We were all wearing seatbelts and we were extremely lucky."

The accident occurred less than three months before the World Championships. Jaynes was held out of practice because of her condition and was pulled from a July tournament in Spain that was a tune-up for the Worlds. "It was a rough time. I was having trouble with my short-term memory. I was worried I wouldn't be cleared to compete."

After six weeks off the mat, Jaynes was cleared to begin training, just over a month before the World Championships. "My condition had improved dramatically by the time I got to Worlds. We had good strategies and game plans, and I felt strong when I competed. My conditioning wasn't at my best because of all the time I had off the mat, but I had a good, positive attitude going into the tournament. I had to wrestle smart and stay in good position. I had to conserve energy when I could — I didn't have a choice because I had missed a lot of training and didn't have the gas tank that I normally have."

Unlike her first two trips to Worlds, Jaynes would be competing in her home country, at the Orleans Arena in Las Vegas. And unlike 2007 and 2012, Jaynes would wrestle as a mother. She came out strong, earning a 10-0 technical fall over Kazakhstan's Madina Bakbergenova before earning a hard-fought 8-5 win over Hungary's Emese Barka. She was one win away from reaching the gold-medal finals, but those hopes quickly vanished in the semifinals. Ukraine's Oksana Herhel caught Jaynes with an early throw and recorded a first-period fall.

"I got caught and got beat. That's sports — you've got to dust yourself off and come back fighting again in the next match. If I had held onto that loss too long, I wouldn't have been able to go back out there and win a medal."

Jaynes' opponent in the bronze-medal match was Azerbaijan's Irina Netreba, 10 years younger. Netreba came out aggressively, turning Jaynes to her back early in the bout with a near-side cradle, but Jaynes quickly broke the lock and broke free from danger.

Down 2-0 at the break, Jaynes countered a shot attempt and eventually came around for a takedown to tie the match 2-2 early in the second period.

That set the stage for a dramatic sequence in the match's final seconds. Netreba shot in on a leg attack and was credited with two points, but Jaynes countered and exposed her opponent's back to the mat for two points. The match ended in a 4-4 deadlock, but Jaynes won by virtue of scoring last.

At long last, Jaynes had landed a spot on the podium. She had won a World bronze medal. A relieved Jaynes smiled while still down on the mat, raising both arms triumphantly as she celebrated her landmark win. She blew a kiss to the crowd as the USA fans roared in approval. Her win also clinched a third-place finish for the American team at the 2015 Worlds.

"I knew it was going to be tough to win that bronze medal, and it was. I needed all of my strength to win that. It was amazing. Right after the match, I thought to myself, 'Oh my God, I finally did this.' It was just pure gratitude. It was so great to do this not only for myself, but to help my team win a trophy."

Coach Steiner said he was proud of the persistence Jaynes showed during her career. "Leigh put in a lot of time. When she first came to Colorado, she was talented but still very, very green. She came a long way and put a lot of effort into her career. Wrestling has helped guide her and give her opportunities she may not have had in her life. It was great to see her win a medal and help the team finish third. That was a huge win for Leigh and a huge win for our team. It's a great story."

Jaynes came up short of her Olympic goal again in 2016 as the U.S. was unable to qualify a wrestler in her weight class. However, her persistence and perseverance did pay off when she earned that elusive World medal in 2015.

It has been a long, but rewarding journey. "I just march to the beat of my own drum," she said after medaling in 2015. "A lot of people said that I was past my prime and that my career was pretty much over. I just refused to believe that. I knew I had the ability to wrestle with the best girls in the world and it became a reality for me.

"I was so proud to be able to win a medal for my country after all I had been through. This sport has done so much for me. Wrestling saved my life."

CHAPTER 13
Adeline Gray

Adeline Gray was just 18 years old when she competed in her first Senior World Championships in 2009, in Herning, Denmark. Even though she was very young for the Senior level, Gray had spent a dozen years on the mat working toward that special moment.

The oldest of four daughters to George and Donna Gray, she was an active young girl with more than an abundance of energy while growing up in Denver, Colorado. At the age of six, Gray joined Bear Creek Junior Wrestling, where her uncle, Paul Delmonico, was the coach. Her father, George, a Denver police officer, also helped coach.

"It was so much fun," Gray said. "I remember having a blast." The first move she learned, an arm bar, was taught to her by her father. That move served her well as she progressed through the youth ranks and eventually onto greatness on the Senior level.

Gray describes herself as being "super-hyper" as a girl. She didn't want to go to bed at night, couldn't sit still through a meal or during class at school. She had to be moving. "Even now, if I don't work out for a couple days, I can feel this buzzing energy. I radiate this overwhelming energy. People are like 'You've just got to stop — you've got to chill out.' It's this craziness that probably is ADHD. My parents were like, 'This kid is going to need to be medicated.'"

If she wasn't ready to go to bed, she would do push-ups and sit-ups until she was so tired or bored that she wanted to go to sleep.

Delmonico's daughter, Arenet, also wrestled, but for the most part Gray was wrestling against boys. She struggled in her earliest matches, but her father

Adeline Gray started wrestling when she was six years old.

encouraged her by setting small goals. She was pinned in her first match, but achieved a goal in the second match by not getting pinned. In the third match, the goal was to score a point and she accomplished that.

By her fourth tournament, Gray had won her first medal, which kick-started a career where she continued winning medals in virtually every tournament she entered. "Wrestling helped calm me down — it helped me burn off a lot of my energy. I was bouncing off the walls all the time, but I would be so exhausted after practice I would finally calm down."

A friend of her father, another police officer, had a son on the team who would practice against Gray. "His son was a little smaller than me — I had like 10 pounds on him." The boy's father approached her at practice and told her, "I'll give you a dollar if you can take my son down."

"I would go ahead and take him down and the father would throw a dollar toward me on the mat," she said. "By the end of practice, I'd have three dollars or so in my pocket."

She tried a number of other sports growing up — cross country, soccer, softball, swimming and tennis. "If you would have asked me my favorite sport until high school, I would have said soccer. I didn't concentrate solely on wrestling until my junior year of high school."

Gray's mother was set on her daugh-

Adeline Gray was a place winner among the boys in Colorado at the age of 12.

ter playing basketball because she was very tall for her age. "My mom kept insisting that I play basketball. I wouldn't say it was a fight, but it was a discussion every year between ages 8-12. Every time I came home exhausted from a wrestling practice she'd often say, 'I can still make you a basketball player.' My mom was a basketball player in college and she was looking to get me into a sport that as a woman I could do long-term."

Gray continued to thrive on the mat. She spent her first three years of high school wrestling against boys, first at Bear Creek High School and then at Chatfield, in the Denver suburbs, where she was named team captain as a junior. "I learned so much in high school, getting beat up, getting the boys to make me better. It was an opportunity for me to have to figure it out. I have girls on the Olympic stage that are stronger than me, girls that are bigger and faster. It definitely feels escalated when you're on the mat against a boy sometimes because those differences are larger. You look at a 140-pound girl, she's going to be softer than the 140-pound boy, especially when he turns 17, 18 years old."

Gray earned the respect of the boys on her team. "I was working very hard and I was winning. Being voted captain was a pretty big deal for me. I remember winning a tournament in Windsor and getting the Outstanding Wrestler award. I think it was the first time a girl had ever won it. I gained a lot of respect and credibility when I won that."

She adjusted well to competing against boys, but there were some challenges involved with it as well. "I was very focused on my wrestling, and I didn't concern myself very much with the bigotry. Columbine High was the biggest problem. The coaches there told the wrestlers, who were all boys, that they didn't have to wrestle girls. The time I was most frustrated was when a particular boy who I was better than wouldn't wrestle me at a tournament.

"A couple of weeks later, I saw the same boy wrestling a first-year girl in another tournament. He was kicking the crap out of her. That made me really angry. It wasn't that he didn't want to wrestle a girl, he didn't want to lose to a girl. I understand we live in a society where a boy thinks it's bad to lose to a girl, but it was terribly disappointing seeing coaches foster the idea of denying a girl a chance to compete. The Columbine coaches stated that girls should not be wrestling."

Gray said there was a boy on her high school team who "shunned me" at practice. "He started dating this girl who didn't like it that he wrestled me in practice. It was the same boy, Jerry, that I had beat out the year before for the 135-pound spot. So he wouldn't wrestle with me.

"Right before districts, the *Denver Post* was coming to a practice to write a feature article on me and our team. When the *Post* came into the room, I was wrestling with Jerry's little brother and Jerry was wrestling with my sister. While in front of the newspaper photographer, our coach yells, 'Switch partners now.' So we switched wrestling partners and Jerry got photographed in the paper wrestling with me after he had avoided contact with me all season. It was kind of funny because I thought it was strange that Jerry's girlfriend would feel the way she did."

There were other issues as well, including what she was wearing to compete. "Adeline once had a referee tell her she couldn't compete because her singlet was different. She was wearing a girl's singlet," said Gray's mother. "Another time, she was told by a referee she couldn't wrestle in a tournament because she was wearing nail polish. The ref thought she might flick it off and get it in another boy's eye. I laughed when he said that because I thought he was kidding."

The referee apparently wasn't kidding. "You have to take that nail polish off before I allow you to wrestle," the referee told Gray. Another official eventually stepped in with a stern message to the referee: "Shut up! That's not a rule. She's allowed to wrestle."

Gray had also been excelling when wrestling against girls while coming up through the USA Wrestling age-group ranks. She recalls a pivotal moment at a women's athletic camp, during a seminar with a world champion swimmer who asked athletes to write down their goals.

"I was 14 or 15 and that camp was hard — they pushed me a lot. I didn't know if I was ready to work that hard, year-round, and fully commit to that lifestyle and dedicate my world to it. The swimmer was insistent that everyone write down, 'I want to be an Olympic champion,' so I stubbornly did so.

"It's interesting that now the only thing I think of when I wake up is, 'I want to be an Olympic champion.' I still have that piece of paper in my room. I didn't believe it then, but I have come full circle. I now know how much this world can offer me and how amazing the opportunities in my life are right now."

Gray won a Junior World title at 67 kilograms/147.5 pounds in 2008 at age 17. She elected to spend her senior year of high school training in freestyle wrestling at the U.S. Olympic Education Center (USOEC) at Northern Michigan University. "I really didn't want to go and leave my Colorado friends for my senior year. However, the opportunity for a full-ride scholarship was a huge deal. My mom was totally against it, but my dad thought it was a good idea for me."

Gray was joined at Northern Michigan by Helen Maroulis, who had placed third at the Junior World Championships in 2008 before competing at her first Senior World Championships at age 17. She was wrestling at 51 kilograms/112 pounds at the time.

Gray and Maroulis became teammates, roommates and classmates. Both attended Marquette High School in Michigan as high-school seniors while training with top young women wrestlers at the USOEC. They spent nine months rooming together in Marquette.

"We both pretty much brought every single thing we owned and put it into this tiny 8x8 room," Gray said. "It was the most crowded place you've ever been. We both thought you were supposed to bring every picture, every stuffed animal."

Gray said it wasn't a memorable experience at Northern Michigan. "Looking back, I wish I hadn't gone. I was miserable. Michigan sucked — it was awful for me. Helen and I fought all the time. We tried to become best friends because we were both in the same situation, but our personalities are totally different. We were forced into the same room, doing the same camps, going to classes together. We never had

Adeline Gray has helped change the perception of female athletes. Jen Gutches

a break from each other. We were ready to kill each other by the end of the year. It was hard for us to swallow our pride sometimes. She won a couple tournaments where I didn't and I started becoming jealous. She helped me step up my game to make the Senior team, and then she didn't make the team in 2009 and I did. We were two of the best girls in Michigan, but our relationship became very competitive.

"I really feel that everything in my life could have happened one year later. I was 17 when I went off. I didn't have a great time and I feel that I kind of got robbed of my senior year of high school."

Gray admits she benefited from her time on the mat. "I did learn a lot when I was in Michigan. I learned how to train twice a day. It was my first formal training in freestyle. I learned how to wrestle par terre [mat wrestling] and understand positioning and the rules of freestyle. That was huge. If you compete on the Senior level, you need to know the rules. And it was my first time away from home."

Gray and Maroulis never did attend Northern Michigan University. Gray returned home and received her high school diploma back in Denver. "It was a strain on our relationship with Helen and I rooming together. But it was good because we were getting thrown into that Senior level of competition and we began to realize what this sport was really about."

That was evident when Gray landed a spot on her first Senior World Team in 2009. With her father in attendance, she came within an eyelash of earning her first World medal at the 2009 World Championships. She stormed out to a big early lead, cranking Nigeria's Ifeoma Iheanacho to her back with an arm bar and nearly pinning her in the first period. The Nigerian somehow avoided the fall and came back to win the final two periods to claim the bronze medal. It was a crushing setback for Gray, who fought back tears after the loss.

She was only 18 and had nearly won a World medal on the Senior level. But that didn't ease the pain for a distraught Gray. "When they didn't call the pin, I think I kind of lost my focus. I had a mental lapse and it cost me the match. That was a good tournament for me because I realized I could compete at the highest level. I knew I could excel against the best in the world."

The ultra-competitive Gray bounced right back. She followed up two months later by winning the New York Athletic Club tournament held at the historic club that sponsors her. She was wrestling well at the World Cup in early 2010 before dislocating her kneecap against Ukraine in the last match of the event.

That injury sidelined Gray for the

rest of 2010 though she came back strong in 2011, earning her first World medal by taking a bronze at 67 kilos in Istanbul, Turkey.

The Olympic year was coming up in 2012 and Gray had a decision to make. Since her weight class of 67 kilograms was not one of the four Olympic weight classes, she had to either bump up a class to 72 kilograms/158.5 pounds or drop down a class to 63 kilograms/138.75 pounds. "In hindsight, it probably would have been best to go up to 72 kilos. I had to lose almost 10 kilos [around 20 pounds] to make 63 kilos. It was a pretty big sacrifice."

Gray made it down to 63 kilograms and advanced to the finals of the 2012 Olympic Trials against Elena Pirozhkova. Competing in front of a sellout crowd of 14,000-plus fans, Pirozhkova beat Gray to earn a trip to the 2012 Olympics. "I did the best I could. Unfortunately, I wasn't able to make the team."

Gray received an opportunity a few months later when the World Championships were held just outside Edmonton, Canada. "It was awesome to have that opportunity. I was sick of feeling sorry for myself. I was very depressed after not making the Olympic team. I had a real pity-party for myself. I was not used to losing and all of a sudden I didn't get that glory. I wanted that limelight, I wanted that success. I had a pretty successful run, had always been successful in meeting my goals and here I was without the opportunity to represent the USA and win an Olympic medal."

Competing back at her normal weight class at 67 kilograms, Gray captured her first World title in September 2012 in Canada. With both of her parents in attendance, Gray pinned Canada's Dori Yeats in the finals. "I was ready and determined. Dori was a year or two younger than me. Her dad was a Greco Olympian. I call it 'my perfect match.' First of all, Terry Steiner, my coach, was in my corner, and he had taught me how to do the back arch and my dad was in the stands and he was the one who taught me the arm drag and the chicken wing.

"So, I end up going out there and I took the girl down with an arm-drag, then she stood up and I got a pike position on her, and picked her up and threw her for four points like Terry had shown me. Then on the mat I bar-armed her and pinned her. It was great because I had my dad there who taught me the base skills and Terry who taught me the high-elevation throws. It was awesome to have it all come full circle. Standing on the podium as the World champion and having everyone there was such a thrill."

A week later, Gray moved up to 72 kilograms and won a University

World title. It set the stage for the next Olympic cycle with Gray permanently moving to the heavyweight division, though she was still not convinced of the weight hike. The international wrestling federation had changed the weight classes, with heavyweight going from 72 kilos to the new class of 75 kilograms/165 pounds. Gray was convinced the new class of 69 kilograms/152 pounds would be a better fit, but Coach Steiner eventually convinced Gray to try 75 kilograms, and she took bronze at the 2013 World Championships in Budapest, Hungary before going undefeated at the 2014 World Cup.

But things weren't going so well off the mat. Gray and Steiner frequently butted heads during the 2013-14 season. "There was a lot of frustration — on her part and on mine," Steiner said. "It wasn't pretty for a while. I was frustrated with her when she wasn't doing things I wanted her to do. We just didn't see eye-to-eye."

During a meeting in Steiner's office, Gray didn't mince words with her coach. "Every time you open your mouth, I feel so much animosity towards you," Gray told Steiner. "I just want to leave the room. I don't want to listen at all."

Steiner was floored. "That hit me hard as a coach. We were supposed to be on the same team. I don't wake up every day thinking, 'How can I piss off Adeline Gray today?' I am really here only for one reason, and that's to help you be successful. My job is to find a way to work together.

"I was surprised with what she was saying. The bottom line was that we needed to find a way through this. We left the room and I was upset — with myself more than anything. I asked myself, 'Why can't I get this right?' It went on like this for a long time. It wasn't a great relationship."

The meeting with Gray was an eye-opener for Steiner. "I came to the realization as a coach that when you are coaching 16-, 17-, 18-year olds it is one thing — you can be more controlling and dictate what you want done, but when you are coaching athletes in their 20s, you need to make them part of the process. It's their career and I don't want to make the decisions for them. They need to make those decisions with good information."

Steiner and Gray still weren't on the same page entering World Team Camp and a six-week training phase before the 2014 Worlds. The team had just returned home to Colorado Springs from a big pre-World event, the Golden Grand Prix in Azerbaijan, where Gray had placed second.

"We were pretty much in the same place as eight months earlier," Steiner said. "We were both still frustrated because we couldn't get it right."

Steiner then gave Gray the U.S.

team's training plan for the next six weeks. He asked her to take it home over the weekend and come up with any changes she felt might help better prepare her for the Worlds.

"Tell me which workouts you don't want to be a part of," Steiner told Gray, "and tell me what you are going to replace them with, and tell me the reason for changing it and what you are doing."

Gray came back and eliminated four mat workouts over a six-week period. "I was worried she would come back with something that didn't look like the same plan, but she didn't do that," Steiner said. "I thought, 'We're having all this stress over four workouts?' Now it didn't seem like anything at all. We made a few other changes, but I saw that it wasn't like she was trying to get out of anything. She just was wanting to preserve her body and make sure she wasn't getting beat up.

"I told her, 'Yes, I can accept this.' As a coach, it was probably the best thing I ever did. I let her make some decisions; I let her be a part of the process. I let her know that her opinion was valued and this was not a dictatorship."

Gray said she knew "that we needed to change something. Terry runs a very Iowa-style room. The Iowa guys are the toughest of the tough. They push to hell and back, and they survive. I'm not built for that. I am a little fragile.

I had to alter how I trained and how I approached my training workouts, so that I could be successful on the mat.

"I told Terry that I wasn't going to compete as much. I'm not going to train as much. I'm going to listen to my body. It was hard to do. I had coaches saying, 'No, that's not the way to go' but Terry was okay with it. He was on my side. My teammates joke that 'I bike my way to World championships' because I'm always on the bike in the training center and not so much on the mat. I got to the point where if I went to practice and my body didn't feel right, I would leave practice and go back to my room to do homework or something."

The changes Steiner and Gray made paid off immediately. Gray followed with a magical performance at the 2014 World Championships in Tashkent, Uzbekistan. She swept through the bottom half of a bracket that included the world's top five ranked wrestlers to reach the gold-medal match, where she opened by pulling out an improbable 11-10 win over Zhou Qian of China in the first round. Gray trailed 9-2 late in the match before scoring a takedown and a succession of leg laces to tie the match 9-9. Zhou came back with a pushout to lead 10-9 before Gray countered a shot and exposed Zhou's back to the mat with six seconds left for two points and a dramatic win.

"I just had to keep fighting," Gray

said. "I gave everything I had and put it all into that match. My experience paid off. I was behind 9-2, but I was still just a few laces away. I knew I still had time to come back."

Gray trailed 6-5 early in the second period before breaking and pinning 2013 World fifth-place finisher Yasemin Adar of Turkey in the second round. Gray, ranked fourth in the world, held off world number two, Hiroe Suzuki of Japan, 2-1 in the quarterfinals, avenging a loss to Suzuki two months earlier in the Golden Grand Prix.

She capped an amazing four-win first session with a 5-1 victory over Epp Mae of Estonia in the semifinals and then defeated Brazil's Aline da Silva 2-1 in the finals. "To be a World champion, you've got to beat the best girls in the world," Gray said that day. "It's an exciting day. I knew it was a gauntlet of a bracket to go through and I woke up this morning and I just decided I was going to win. My coaches really believed in me."

Steiner credited Gray's resiliency and composure in her brilliant first-session run. "Adeline had a gutsy, gutsy performance. Down 9-2 against China, she came back and showed why she's a true champion. She won very tough matches against very strong opponents."

Gray's performance capped a turbulent, trying season where coach and athlete effectively addressed their issues and came up with a solution. "Everyone was happy," Steiner said. "For me, I learned that at a certain point in time you have to step back as a coach and really listen to the athlete and learn from them and respect what they are asking. Since that time, we haven't had a problem. We've had a great relationship. I put more of it on me than on Adeline. I needed to loosen the reins a little bit. She has performed well and hasn't been a jerk. I'm getting what I want, she's getting what she wants and together we are all getting what we want."

Said Gray: "I felt better about my training and preparedness for the Worlds than ever before. My body felt great going into the tournament."

The 5-foot-11 Gray finally came to the realization that 75 kilograms was her weight class. "The girls were not bigger and stronger than I was. The weight class became a good fit for me."

Gray has developed a penchant for competing her best when the stakes are highest. "Adeline loves that spotlight," Steiner said. "Some people, they want to win and do their thing, but they don't want that spotlight and that kind of attention. Adeline, I think she revels in it. She's a professional athlete. She knows what her job is. I don't have to worry about Adeline as far as doing what she needs to be doing. She's very self-driven and self-motivated. She knows what's at stake."

Gray also is as hard-nosed and resilient as any athlete when she competes. "It's the tenacity and toughness that they see," she said after a win at the Beat the Streets dual in New York City in 2016. "I don't think women always are portrayed as tough. When you go out there, you have to be tough. You have to be brave. You have to really believe in yourself to step on that mat and have the confidence to win. And I think that's something that girls are drawn to. They realize how important confidence is in so many areas of their lives."

Afsoon Roshanzamir Johnston, a 2016 Olympic coach, said women like Gray have helped change the perception of women athletes. "We're at that age where femininity has been redefined. You can see a very tough woman — with muscles, with strength, with endurance — battling, and that's still feminine. Because of that, I think women's wrestling is going to gain more attention and popularity and support."

Gray captured her third World title at the 2015 World Championships in Las Vegas. She beat da Silva and Qian again, this time in the semifinals and finals, en route to her third World title. Tricia Saunders, with four gold medals, is the only American with more World titles than Gray now. "It's a real thrill to be able to win a World title on America soil," Gray said after winning in Vegas.

"Now I'm ready to go win that gold medal at the Olympics."

She followed up by making her first U.S. Olympic team after rolling to the championship at the 2016 trials in April. "This is a dream come true, but I have bigger goals," she said that day. "I'm ready to win an Olympic gold medal for the United States of America. I'm ready to do it."

CHAPTER 14
Helen Maroulis

Helen Maroulis was a 17-year-old high school student who was halfway around the world from home when she stepped onto the mat in Tokyo, Japan for her first Senior World Championships in October 2008.

Maroulis won her first match by fall before being thrown right into the fire, against lightweight legend Hitomi Sakamoto of Japan. Maroulis was swept in two straight periods by the dynamic and technically sound Sakamoto, who finished her remarkable career with eight World titles and an Olympic gold medal. "It was a great experience for me and a great opportunity to compete on that level at such a young age," Maroulis said. "I learned a lot on that trip, plus I received the chance to wrestle the best girl in the world. I just tried to take it all in and gain as much I could from the experience. It definitely motivated me to want to get back there."

Maroulis had placed third at the Junior World Championships in 2008 before competing at her first Senior Worlds later that year, even though she still had a year left of high school. She was wrestling at 51 kilograms/112 pounds.

Maroulis almost didn't even make it to this point after nearly giving up the sport for good a few years before. She followed an interesting path to becoming one of the world's elite wrestlers. Helen's father, John, was born in Greece and came to the United States when he was 12 years old. "His goal in life was to make it out of poverty. It was a big adjustment when he came to the U.S. It was the first time he had seen electricity."

Her father went to high school in Maryland — after being bullied in

Helen Maroulis almost gave up wrestling on several occasions.

Helen Maroulis learned to wrestle in the state of Maryland, not usually recognized as a

ing powerhouse. John Sachs

school, he took up wrestling. He earned a college scholarship to a school in Pennsylvania, but turned it to down so he could work and earn money for his family. "He met my mom [Paula] when he was 21, and they married a year later. He went to work because he didn't want his kids to starve like he did."

Maroulis has an older brother, Michael, and a younger brother, Tony. Both boys played baseball. Tony started wrestling when he was six. "I would sit in the corner of the wrestling room and watch Tony wrestle at practice. He didn't have a partner one day, so my mom asked me to come and practice with Tony. That got me started. Within two weeks, I was going to all of the practices and doing all the pushups and sprints. But I was not able to compete.

"Before wrestling, I tried ballet and gymnastics. I was very shy. The instructors told my mom not to bring me back. I would avoid eye contact with the instructors — I mostly put my head down and cried. That didn't happen with wrestling. I truly believe that I was destined to be a wrestler."

The local middle school had no wrestling team, so Maroulis learned and developed her early wrestling skills through the Maryland club system.

Before her first competitive match, her dad made a deal with her. "You can keep wrestling if you win your first match," he told his daughter. She won her first match, but struggled that first season as a 60-pounder, competing for the Gaithersburg Sports Association Club. "I ended up my first year with something like 30 losses," she said. "That was pretty rough."

After her first year of wrestling, Maroulis said her parents made her quit the sport. "They told me there was no future in the sport for girls, and that I shouldn't have to only wrestle boys."

Soon after that, an announcement came in September 2001 that women's wrestling was being added to the Olympic Games program in 2004. "That gave me another chance. I wanted to be an Olympian in wrestling."

Maroulis made huge gains on the mat in her second season, finishing with a winning record. "I went into the Beltway League competition that year. This was the first time I encountered negativity from guys on other teams — snide remarks, forfeits. I was suppose to wrestle for the Gaithersburg Eagles in an advanced league but some of the coaches' primary objectives were to get me to quit.

"My mom emailed this one coach, Mike DeSarno, asking if he'd coach me. He said, 'No, I don't coach women.' Then he saw me wrestle and right away got back to my mom with, 'Okay, bring her over to my practices in Mount Airy'. My mom drove me there four times a week — it's an hour drive each way — because I was liking it so much."

Mount Airy was a top team in the state and Maroulis was the only girl on the team. "The other two team coaches were against my being there, but Mike told them, 'Here's the deal — you have to accept her. She's going to be good.'"

That progression continued when Maroulis became the first girl to qualify for the Maryland state tournament as a Magruder High School freshman at 112 pounds. She also became the first girl to place at state, finishing in sixth place in 2006. She went 33-9 that season while competing against boys. "I had to be more flexible and technical than the boys to overcome their strength."

She finished with a 3-3 record at the 2006 Maryland state tournament, where no female had won a match before that year. Nicole Woody, who Maroulis had trained with and become friends with, went 1-2 at 103 pounds that year at the same state meet. "I was hoping to win a match, and I was hoping to place," Maroulis said in 2006. "That was my goal and that's what I did. I'm happy with myself for the most part, but no one likes losing. There are guys who are freshmen who are in the finals. If I'm going to be treated like one of the guys, I kind of want to be looked at in that view."

Max Sartoph, Maroulis' coach at Magruder, came away impressed. "We have had guys here who were state

High school roommates Maroulis and Gray won World golds in 2015. Tony Rotundo

champions who didn't place at state as freshmen," Sartoph said. "You think about all of the good wrestlers, and Helen's already doing better than a lot of them did at this age. It's an awesome accomplishment for her."

Maroulis opened the state tournament with a win over Chesapeake's Jarrid Bosque before meeting him again later in the tournament. She dropped a close match to Bosque in the fifth-place bout. "She's good, man, especially as a freshman," Bosque said of Maroulis after the tournament. "Usually freshmen, they don't go far. It's very rare that you get a freshman that can place, and she's a girl. She could be first next year, or her junior or senior year. She's going to be good."

Sartoph said Maroulis was accepted early on by the teammates on her high school team. "Everyone knew that she wrestled and that she was very good," Sartoph said. "I graduated from high school in 1991, and we had a girl on our wrestling team. Back then, there was a lot of discussion and flak about girls competing in the sport. But now, it doesn't seem like it's so new anymore."

"People have said things like, 'you're really good for a girl.' It would be great if everyone could look past the girl factor," Maroulis said during her junior season. "My teammates and coaches already have."

Maroulis encountered many of the same obstacles that girls faced while competing against boys in a male-dominated sport — there were times when other teams forfeited matches against Maroulis because of her gender. "It happened numerous times during my freshman and my sophomore year. It's a bigger insult than most people think because I practice very hard, I love to compete and I push myself to help my team. I guess some coaches don't want their wrestlers losing to a girl, but it's not fair, it's very disrespectful and it bugs me a lot."

Maroulis also dealt with her share of admirers while competing in high school. "This guy came up to me at a tournament and said, 'My friend wants your phone number,'" she said. "That happened a few times."

She became less intimidated as she continued to stockpile wins against boys. "I remember we were up at a tournament at Hagerstown," Sartoph said. "So here's this pretty young girl wrestling against this big, strong guy with muscles and tattoos who looked like a monster. And Helen beat this kid."

Maroulis won a hard-fought battle in overtime, and the crowd erupted with a loud ovation. "That kid looked very mean and I was nervous for her going into that match," Sartoph said. "People got to see what Helen was all about during that match. She was very confident, didn't get nervous and beat a very good, intimidating wrestler."

Maroulis faced the same opponent from Williamsport again, and beat him again later in the same tournament. She won by fall in overtime. "Helen finished third in the tournament, but the coaches were so impressed she was named Outstanding Wrestler, which is unheard of," Sartoph said. "That award always goes to a wrestler who wins the tournament."

Maroulis said, "The thing I like about wrestling is you don't have to be tall, or short. Some are strong, powerful wrestlers and some are more technical. You have to be versatile and that's why I love it."

Maroulis suffered a herniated disc in her back as a sophomore and the consensus among doctors was that she should give up wrestling. She was also diagnosed with Lyme's disease. She eventually returned to the mat and qualified again for state, but went 0-2.

Maroulis placed sixth again at state as a junior. At the same time, she was excelling in numerous national events while competing against girls. That is when she was offered a chance to train at the U.S. Olympic Education Center at Northern Michigan as a high school senior. "My dad was against it and my mom was for it. It was tough to leave home. I moved away from home and I also had to leave my boyfriend."

Maroulis then joined another top young wrestler, Adeline Gray, at Northern Michigan, where they were roommates and teammates.

The Michigan experience was difficult for Maroulis. "I was never off on my own before. The weather was bad. We had daily 5am practices and a 9pm curfew. It was a very strict environment. On the other hand, there were good things. It was the first time that I wrestled freestyle exclusively and the first time I wrestled women exclusively. It was a positive stepping stone for my wrestling career. I would do it all over again."

Maroulis moved up a weight class to 55 kilograms/121 pounds after 2008 and didn't make another Senior World team for three years. She started hitting her stride while turning 20 during an exceptional 2011 season. She won a silver medal at the Junior Worlds and placed fifth at the Senior Worlds to qualify the U.S. for the 2012 Olympics in her weight class. She followed by beating Canada's Tonya Verbeek, an eventual three-time Olympic medalist, in the finals of the 2011 Pan American Games.

"Competing in the Olympics has been a dream of mine since I was eight," Maroulis said in the summer of 2011. "I have no idea why wrestling hooked me, but I'm obviously glad that it did."

She was on a roll and was favored to make the Olympic team in 2012. With just four Olympic weight classes, wrestlers were dropping down from the division of 59 kilograms/130 pounds to compete in the Olympic category of 55 kilograms.

One of those wrestlers dropping down was Kelsey Campbell, who had placed fifth at the 2010 Worlds at 59 kilograms. Campbell won the Olympic Trials Challenge Tournament to earn a shot at Maroulis in the best-of-3 series in the trials finals. The winner would represent the United States at the 2012 Olympics.

Campbell came out and won the first match in three periods. She followed with a three-period triumph in the second match and broke down in tears as she earned her spot on the team. Maroulis was also overcome, fighting back tears after a devastating setback.

Shortly after the Olympics, Maroulis entered the World Championships, held just outside Edmonton, Canada. It was an opportunity for wrestlers like Maroulis to rebound from crushing setbacks at the trials. She came out determined and advanced to the finals at 55 kilos, where she faced a daunting opponent in her gold-medal bout — Saori Yoshida of Japan, widely considered the best women's wrestler of all time.

A large group of Japanese media were in Canada to document Yoshida's pursuit of a record-setting 10th World title. But even though Maroulis was a huge underdog, she didn't back down from Yoshida. Maroulis came out with an aggressive game plan, but came up short as Yoshida won by a second-period fall to earn her historic title.

It was still a big day for Maroulis. She had won her first Senior World medal and the 21-year-old gained a huge amount of experience heading into the next Olympic cycle. "My day didn't end the way I wanted it to, but I still had a very good day," Maroulis said after the loss to Yoshida. "I was confident, and I just embraced the battle and I enjoyed it until the last match. I learned so much.

"I wasn't even sure if I was going to wrestle in this event after what happened at the trials. I've had so much support from my coaches, and my family and friends, and they encouraged me to wrestle at the Worlds. I'm so glad I decided to compete here. I learned from my losses and I'm a lot better wrestler now."

Maroulis continued to excel during the next four-year cycle as she looked to build momentum heading into the 2016 Olympics. She won a bronze medal at the 2014 Worlds and entered the 2015 championship in Las Vegas as one of the favorites to win gold at 55 kilograms/121 pounds. A win there not only would give her that elusive first World title, but also provide a springboard as she pursued her first berth on an American Olympic team.

Maroulis rolled into the finals, using a lethal combination of skill and speed.

She then overpowered Russia's Irina Ologonova by an 11-0 technical fall in the finals. A smiling Maroulis ran around the mat holding an American flag above her head in celebration. At age 23, she was on top of the world. "It's a dream come true," Maroulis said. "It's great to see all of the hard work and the sacrifices that I've made pay off."

Late that night, Maroulis and Gray wore broad smiles as they posed together for photographers with their gold medals. "It was awesome for both of us to be able to win World titles in our home country," Maroulis said. "I'll never forget it."

Maroulis has continued to flourish under the coaching of Valentin Kalika, a native of the Ukraine who is based in California. After winning her World title, she still had plenty of work to do to realize her Olympic dream. She had won her 2015 World title at the non-Olympic weight class of 55 kilograms/121 pounds, won the Olympic Trials at 53 kilograms/116.5 pounds and then had to travel overseas two weeks later to win an Olympic Games qualifier in Mongolia. An excited Maroulis raised both arms in victory, clenching both hands in a fist while a wide smile spread across her face. She was a U.S. Olympian.

"Rarely do I show my true emotions on the mat," Maroulis wrote on Facebook that night. "Today was one of those days. I'm truly overjoyed."

Steiner said he talked to Maroulis about how far she had progressed when they went for an evening walk before the Olympic qualifier in Mongolia. "2012 was the best thing that ever happened to you," Steiner told her. "You might not want to hear that, but it really was. Sometimes you have to hit that rock bottom before you really establish yourself."

A few weeks after Maroulis made her first Olympic team, Steiner reflected on her journey. "Helen came back really strong after that setback and took control of her career. She is wrestling at a high level and is at the peak of her career. She has definitely put herself in position to make a run at an Olympic title. I wouldn't count her out."

CHAPTER 15
Rio de Janeiro: The 2016 Olympics

History was about to be made on August 18, 2016 at the Olympic Games in Rio de Janeiro, Brazil. Olympic Park's Carioca Arena 2 was jammed with 6,000 enthusiastic fans for the women's freestyle wrestling finals. Fans were clapping, music was blaring, and flags of the United States and Japan were on full display throughout the venue.

A chant of "U-S-A, U-S-A" could even be heard near matside in the first rows of the stands. The finalists in the 53 kilograms (116.5 pounds) weight category were announced: "From the United States of America," announcer Jason Bryant boomed to the crowd, "Helen Maroulis."

"And from Japan," Bryant followed, "Saori Yoshida."

More than 100 accredited media from Japan, mostly photographers, were there to capture this landmark moment. A large crowd of fans gathered to witness a rare and magical feat.

Yoshida struck gold at the first Olympic Games for women's wrestling in 2004 in Athens, Greece, followed by a second gold in Beijing in 2008, and made it three in London in 2012. She also won a record 13 World titles and had never lost a match in an Olympic Games or a World Championships in a span of 15 years.

The day before, Japanese teammate Kaori Icho had become the first woman in any sport to become a four-time Olympic gold medalist. She was one of three Japanese to win gold medals that day. But even with all of Icho's success, Yoshida, even at 33, was widely recognized as the best women's wrestler on the planet. She was riding a 119-match winning streak, but had looked vulnerable at times during that span and had pulled out a number of close matches in

Elena Pirozhkova and Haley Augello at the Beat-the-Streets matches in Times Square prior to the 2016 Olympics. John Sachs

recent years.

Yoshida was facing a very capable opponent in the 24-year-old Maroulis, who had won World gold, silver and bronze medals. Maroulis had been pinned in two previous meetings against Yoshida, including the 2012 World finals. The first time Maroulis wrestled Yoshida, she was a teenager. She was pinned in 69 seconds and tore a ligament in her elbow.

Two years earlier, Maroulis had practiced with Yoshida and other Japanese wrestlers at a training camp. Maroulis said she failed to score a takedown.

Maroulis had won a World title in 2015, but it was in the non-Olympic weight class of 55 kilograms, while Yoshida won at the Olympic division of 53 kilos.

Maroulis had a tough road to the finals in Rio. She rolled to a pair of technical falls before running into North Korea's Myong Suk Jong in the quarterfinals. Maroulis trailed 4-2 before rallying for a dramatic and gritty 7-4 win. She then followed with an impressive semifinal pin over World champion Sofia Mattsson of Sweden. After that win, Coach Valentin Kalika stopped in the mixed zone interview area to talk about Maroulis. "Helen is ready to win the

Olympics," Kalika said matter-of-factly. "We've trained to beat Yoshida. We have a game plan and we just need to follow it. Yoshida's a great champion, but she's not invincible."

National Coach Terry Steiner echoed those sentiments. "Helen is ready to wrestle on this stage — she won't be overwhelmed and she won't be intimidated. She's ready to have a great performance in the finals."

There was plenty riding on the 5-foot-3 Maroulis' shoulders. Not only was she facing a legend in Yoshida, she was trying to become the first American woman to win an Olympic gold medal in women's freestyle wrestling.

If there were nerves, they didn't show — Maroulis confidently bounced onto the elevated platform for the biggest match of her life. She displayed the same confident, business-like demeanor she had on her road to the finals even though she was facing an opponent competing in her fourth Olympic final.

The whistle blew to start the match, and there were few risks taken by either wrestler in the first three minutes. Down 1-0 after the first period, after conceding a passivity point, Maroulis kept her composure and didn't panic. She fought off a pair of leg attack attempts by Yoshida by demonstrating superb defense.

Maroulis used a nifty throw-by maneuver to spin behind Yoshida for a two-point takedown early in the second period. She appeared to score a one-point pushout with a minute left, but drove Yoshida off her feet for a two-point takedown to lead 4-1.

The mat judge and chairman both confirmed the takedown and Japan elected not to challenge the call.

Maroulis was on the verge of making history of her own by becoming the first U.S. female wrestler to win an Olympic gold medal. As time ran out, she became overcome with emotion. She hugged Kalika, the coach who had elevated her wrestling to new heights over the past three years. "Valentin believed in me and he instilled the confidence in me that I could beat anybody. His dream was to coach an Olympic champion and we both accomplished our dreams."

During this Olympic cycle, Maroulis also trained with and was coached by Seiko Yamamoto, who won four World titles while wrestling for Japan.

Maroulis ran around the mat holding an American flag above her head in celebration after the landmark win in Rio. "It's an incredible feeling to do this — it hasn't really sunk in yet but it's just amazing to win a gold medal. It's a dream come true. This means so much to do this because I've made so many sacrifices and worked so hard to get to this point."

The win drew comparisons to American Rulon Gardner's stunning Olympic

Terry Steiner coached an Olympic gold medalist at the 2016 Games.

and focus on my game plan. We've been working on preparing for this match for a year and it paid off."

Twelve years earlier, American Sara McMann had a second-period lead in the first Olympic women's finals in 2004 before Icho rallied for her first of four Olympic titles. "It's been a long, long road," said Steiner, who became National Coach in 2002. "It's very satisfying to finally accomplish this. It didn't come easy by any means, but it was worth it. I can't say enough for what Helen did to become our first Olympic champion. She definitely deserves this."

Maroulis and Yoshida both fell to the mat just a few feet away from each other as the match ended while being overcome by emotion. "I really hope this puts women's wrestling on the map," Maroulis said. "I think wrestling can become more popular and I think it can grow. With this gold medal, girls in the United States now realize what they can achieve in this sport. Hopefully, it inspires more young girls to get into wrestling. I was a very shy and timid kid when I was real young and wrestling helped me gain confidence. You can benefit so much from this sport."

Maroulis has received her share of recognition for her Olympic win. She appeared on NBC's *Today* show the day after her win, and she received extensive media coverage in *USA Today*, the *Los Angeles Times* and the *Washington*

Greco-Roman finals upset over three-time gold medalist Alexander Karelin of Russia in the 2000 Olympics.

"Saori Yoshida is the greatest champion in our sport and has set the bar extremely high," Steiner said. "For Helen Maroulis to beat her is an outstanding accomplishment. This has been a long time coming and we're happy to finally get this monkey off our back."

Yoshida broke down in tears after the loss, and was still crying during the medal ceremony and post-match press conference. "Yoshida is a great champion and what she's accomplished is really impressive," Maroulis said. "I have dreamed so much about wrestling in this match. I was able to stay in the moment

Adeline Gray misses out on her first attempt at an Olympic medal. Tony Rotundo

A magical moment for Helen Maroulis in Rio de Janeiro. John Sachs

Golden girl Helen Maroulis with her fellow Olympic medal winners in 2016. John Sachs

Post. She was honored at a Washington Nationals and Baltimore Orioles baseball game shortly after returning home from Rio. Both the First Lady Michelle Obama and Democratic Presidential Nominee Hilary Clinton congratulated Maroulis on Twitter after her victory.

"I was shocked to see that," Maroulis said. "To know that those people paid attention to women's wrestling and saw that history was made, and took time to Tweet about it, that is so awesome. To see some recognition from these very prominent individuals is really cool."

Winning a gold medal also will add a significant boost to Maroulis' bank account. She was awarded $25,000 from the US Olympic Committee and $250,000 from the Living the Dream Medal Fund for winning an Olympic gold medal in wrestling.

Maroulis knows she now has an opportunity to promote her sport even more after her landmark accomplishment. "It was never my goal to become the first American woman to win gold. But now that that's done, I do feel like there's a responsibility, a platform I can use to build the sport.

Three-time World champion Adeline Gray, who many expected to become the first Olympic women's wrestling champion in U.S. history, came up short of winning a medal at 165 pounds in Rio. The top-ranked Gray, a first-time Olympian, suffered a last-second 4-1 setback to three-time world bronze medalist Vasalisa Marzaliuk of Belarus. She was eliminated when the third-ranked Marzaliuk lost in the semifinals.

"It's disappointing and it's heartbreaking," said Gray. "I overlooked that girl and obviously I shouldn't overlook a girl who has World and Olympic medals. I beat that girl nine out of 10 times, but it didn't happen today. I got defensive and was just trying to protect my lead."

In Gray's setback, Marzaliuk turned Gray to her back with one second left in the match to earn the victory. The match was tied 1-1 with Gray holding the advantage because of a passivity call on Marzaliuk. "We were probably too conservative, especially early in the match where we could've opened it up more," Steiner said. "We started the match with too slow of a pace. Then at the end we just let her in there too easily and she was able to score. We just didn't open up and we needed better tactics."

Gray had won 39 consecutive matches before the loss in Rio. This was her first loss since 2014. "This probably hasn't really sunk in yet and it will take a while to sink in," Gray said just moments after being eliminated. "It's definitely a different feeling. I haven't had a loss in a long time.

Gray, 25, is a five-time world medalist. She won world titles in 2012, 2014 and 2015. "I know I'm still one of the best girls in the world and I've proven that on a pretty consistent basis. It's unfortunate that today just wasn't that day. You only get this opportunity once every four years and you have to get the job done."

The top-seeded Gray had won by a quick first-round fall over Colombia's Andrea Olaya Gutierrez, who was fifth in the 2014 and 2015 World Championships. "I had a great training camp and I felt good coming in here. It just didn't happen for me today."

Gray said she wasn't sure if she was going to commit to wrestling in the next four-year Olympic cycle. Steiner credited Gray for the contributions she's made to the U.S. women's program. "Adeline had very high expectations — this is not going to be easy to live with. It's going to take some time, but life goes on. If Adeline Gray wants to continue on, there's more chances for her. She's won a lot of championships and a lot of titles. She's still a great champion."

Gray was one of the first people to congratulate Maroulis after she won Olympic gold. Their careers have paralleled each other since they started wrestling in the same age-group tournaments in their early teens.

"I am so proud and honored to call Helen Maroulis my teammate," Gray wrote on Twitter. "Happy that Team USA has an amazing representative for our first Olympic gold."

Maroulis credited Gray for what she's done for the sport. "I really felt bad for

Adeline because I know that feeling. You put in work for four years and you have this dream. But I think she handled it amazingly. Adeline did a really good job of getting women's wrestling out there before the Games. It's unfortunate how the tournament went for her, but I don't think that has anything to do with what she's accomplished or what kind of wrestler she is or what kind of person she is. I fully expect that she's going to come back stronger than ever."

World champion and four-time World medalist Elena Pirozhkova charged into the Olympic semifinals after knocking off returning World champion Battsetseg Soronzonbold of Mongolia, but she dropped her next two bouts to finish fifth after falling in the bronze-medal match at 138.75 pounds. She fell short of placing for the second straight Olympics.

"It's tough — I came in here ready to win a medal and it just didn't happen. I had a really good training camp and I felt great coming in here. It just wasn't my day, I guess."

Newcomer Haley Augello, 21, showed she definitely belongs on the Olympic stage in giving a great effort. The past Cadet World champion was one win away from competing in the bronze-medal match at 105.5 pounds. She fell just short of a medal match after dropping a 3-2 decision to Kazakhstan's Zhuldyz Eshimova.

Clarissa Chun was an Olympian in 2008 and 2012, but just fell short for 2016

"It's a heartbreak when you train so hard for something," Augello said. "I learned a lot. It was an amazing experience. I lost some matches on a few mistakes, and I was rushing things and wasn't patient. Wrestling in this tournament, I realized I'm right up there with the best of them."

Augello opened with a dominant 7-0 victory over 2015 World bronze medalist Jessica Blaszka of the Netherlands, coming out aggressively in controlling the match from start to finish. She then dropped an 11-2 decision to three-time World champion and top seed Eri Tosaka of Japan in the quarterfinals. Augello actually scored on a takedown to lead 2-1 with two minutes left in the match, but Tosaka countered a turn attempt and reversed Augello to her back to gain control.

Tosaka went on to win an Olympic title. "I was wrestling aggressively and I made a mistake that cost me," Augello said. "I was trying to turn her and slipped off and then she was able to go right to a leg lace."

Augello made the U.S. Olympic team by turning in the biggest surprise of the Olympic Trials — winning a loaded weight class at 105.5 pounds.

That weight class included World champion and Olympic bronze medalist Clarissa Chun, two-time World bronze medalist Alyssa Lampe and World fifth-place finisher Victoria Anthony. Chun had made the Olympics in 2008 and 2012 in that division. She beat Lampe to make the 2012 Olympic team.

Augello had cut down a weight class after previously competing at 116.5 pounds. Seeded fourth in the Challenge Tournament, Augello knocked off the top-seeded Lampe in a gritty 7-6 semifinal victory. She then advanced to face the second-seeded Anthony in the best-of-3 finals.

Anthony earned an impressive 9-2 semifinal win over Chun, who was trying to make her third straight Olympic team. At that point, Anthony was clearly the favorite to make the 2016 Olympic team, but Augello had other ideas.

Augello stormed out strong to take a 6-4 win over the smaller Anthony in the first match of the best-of-3 finals series. The explosive and powerful Anthony rebounded to take the second bout 11-6.

"After the second match, I knew I had to make some changes," Augello said. "I kind of relaxed a little bit after the second match and I knew I had to pick up the pace again for the third match. I had to get back to wrestling with that intensity that I normally compete with. I was able to get back to my style in the last match and show what I can do."

Augello kept her cool and pulled out an 8-2 win in the third bout. "I'm feeling happy, but my goals haven't been achieved yet. I'm not ecstatic because I still have to qualify the weight for the Olympics. I'm obviously happy, but I have to stay ready and get ready to compete again to qualify the weight."

With the weight class still not qualified for the Olympics, Augello traveled to Mongolia and came through less than two weeks after the trials to qualify the United States and herself for a trip to Rio.

"My goal is to win the Olympics," Augello said in April 2016. "I've always set my goals high, and that's what I'm shooting for. I want to win a gold medal."

Although the Olympics field expanded from four to six weight classes for women's wrestling in 2016, the USA only qualified in four weights, falling short at 128 pounds and 152 pounds.

It was fitting that Afsoon Roshanzamir, the first World medalist for the U.S. in women's wrestling in 1989, served as one of the 2016 Olympic coaches for Team USA. "Competing in the Olympics was something I always wanted to do my entire life. The timing just wasn't right," she said prior to the Olympics. "To have it happen where I have the opportunity to go as a coach now, it is really neat. It has come full circle. Now I get to enjoy the whole experience of the Olympics, without the nerves associated with competing in it."

Roshanzamir celebrated her 44th birthday on August 16, 2016, the day before the Olympic wrestling tournament for women's freestyle. "Afsoon being selected as the 2016 Olympic coach is a perfect match," said Marie Ziegler. "It kind of ties everything together because she was there in the beginning."

Gray has also worked closely with Afsoon in recent years. "She is a huge inspiration for us," Gray said. "She had to fight through so many boundaries. She is such a great example about how we need to keep fighting for equity. It's great to see her back involved with the women's program again. She's still having a big impact on the sport."

The first U.S. Olympic gold medal winner in women's wrestling, Helen Maroulis, gained a new perspective on her accomplishment shortly after the drama concluded.

"Before, I put the Olympics on this giant pedestal," Maroulis said. "I felt like it's something that I couldn't reach. I couldn't get. Now that I'm here, I'm like, 'Oh, normal people can win the Olympics. I did that? That's me! Oh, this is so weird and this is so cool and what an honor.' And I thought only the Gods won or something. So that part hasn't sunk in yet. And I don't want to think of myself any differently because of it."

America's first Olympic gold medal winner in women's wrestling. John Sachs

APPENDIX 1

U.S. Women World Championship Medalists

Sandra Bacher............... GOLD 1999 / SILVER 1997 / BRONZE 1998
Ali Bernard..................... BRONZE 2011
Jackie Berube .... SILVER 1996
Clarissa Chun .... GOLD 2008
Asia DeWeese................ SILVER 1989
Katie Downing............... BRONZE 2005, 2007
Tina George .... SILVER 2002, 2003
Adeline Gray .... GOLD 2012, 2014, 2015 / BRONZE 2011, 2013
Leigh Jaynes .... BRONZE 2015
Leia Kawaii .... SILVER 1989
Alyssa Lampe .... BRONZE 2012, 2013
Margaret LeGates .... SILVER 1994
Kristie Marano............... GOLD 2000, 2003 / SILVER 1996, 1997, 1998, 1999, 2007 / BRONZE 2002, 2006
Helen Maroulis .... GOLD 2015 / SILVER 2012 / BRONZE 2014
Sara McMann .... SILVER 2003 / BRONZE 2005, 2007
Patricia Miranda............ SILVER 2000, 2003 / BRONZE 2006
Toccara Montgomery..... SILVER 2001, 2003
Tatiana Padilla .... BRONZE 2008, 2010
Elena Pirozhkova .... GOLD 2012 / SILVER 2010, 2014 / BRONZE 2013
Sally Roberts .... BRONZE 2003, 2005
Afsoon Roshanzamir ..... SILVER 1990 / BRONZE 1989
Tricia Saunders .... GOLD 1992, 1996, 1998, 1999 / SILVER 1993
Iris Smith....................... GOLD 2005
Shannon Williams.......... SILVER 1991, 1993, 1994, 1997
Jenny Wong .... BRONZE 2003
Marie Ziegler .... SILVER 1990, 1991
Vickie Zummo................ BRONZE 1995

APPENDIX 2

U.S. Women Wrestling Olympians

2004

Patricia Miranda	48 kilograms	BRONZE MEDAL
Tela O'Donnell	55 kilograms	
Sara McMann	63 kilograms	SILVER MEDAL
Toccara Montgomery	72 kilograms	

2008

Clarissa Chun	48 kilograms	
Marcie Van Dusen	55 kilograms	
Randi Miller	63 kilograms	BRONZE MEDAL
Ali Bernard	72 kilograms	

2012

Clarissa Chun	48 kilograms	BRONZE MEDAL
Kelsey Campbell	55 kilograms	
Elena Pirozhkova	63 kilograms	
Ali Bernard	72 kilograms	

2016

Haley Augello	48 kilograms	
Helen Maroulis	53 kilograms	GOLD MEDAL
Elena Pirozhkova	63 kilograms	
Adeline Gray	75 kilograms	

APPENDIX 3

Female Wrestlers Competing in U.S. High Schools Participation Statistics from the National Federation of State High School Association

1986-87............**18**

1990-91............**132**

1994-95............**804**

1998-99............**2,361**

2002-03............**3,769**

2006-07............**5,048**

2010-11............**7,351**

2014-15............**11,496**

2015-16............**13,496**

APPENDIX 4

Women's Intercollegiate Varsity Teams
WCWA programs (Freestyle)

Adrian College
Bacone College
Campbellsville University
Eastern Oregon University
Emmanuel College
Ferrum College
King University
Life University
Lindenwood University – Belleville
Lindenwood University – St. Charles
Lyon College
MacMurray College
McKendree University
Menlo College
Midland University
Missouri Baptist University
Missouri Valley College
Oklahoma City University
Ottawa University
Pacific University
Southern Oregon University
The University of the Cumberlands
University of Jamestown
Waldorf College
Warner Pacific College
Wayland Baptist University

Note: There are also several junior college teams in the U.S. that participate within the WCWA program. In addition to these schools, there are nearly 100 U.S. colleges that have a women's club wrestling team. For a list of those participating in their annual NCWA tournament in March, 2016 go to ncwa.net/news/2016/complete-results-of-finals-rounds-at-ncwa-championships.

ABOUT THE AUTHORS

Craig Sesker has been one of the most recognized wrestling writers in the United States and worldwide over the past two decades. Sesker has written two books on wrestling, *Bobby Douglas* and *Driven to Excellence*, and also co-authored a third book, *Saving Wrestling*, with Jamie Moffatt. He has written about wrestling extensively for the *Omaha World-Herald* and USA Wrestling and covered the wrestling competition at his third straight Olympic Games in 2016. Sesker is a two-time National Wrestling Writer of the Year. He resides in Colorado Springs, Colorado.

This is Jamie Moffatt's sixth book to be published on the sport of wrestling. In 2010 he received the prestigious Bob Dellinger Award as the Wrestling Writer of the Year. Moffatt was one of two writers to receive the initial Jay Hammond Memorial Recognition Award in 2014 for his work on the book *Saving Wrestling*. Moffatt is a graduate of Cornell University and is the former Chairman of the EIWA Hall of Fame Committee. He retired after a long career as a Management Consulting Partner for PricewaterhouseCoopers (PwC) in 2000. He resides in Cape May, New Jersey.